The father of three girls, Daniel Petre AO is also one of Australia's most successful technology and media executives. He spent nine years in senior roles with Microsoft Corporation both in Australia and at headquarters in the U.S.

In 1997 Daniel joined PBL (Publishing and Broadcasting Ltd) as Executive Chairman of Ecorp and a Director of PBL. After five years Daniel left Ecorp as the company began its privatisation process.

Since leaving Ecorp Daniel has founded the Petre Foundation with his wife Carolyn and he now splits his time between charitable causes, private equity investments, strategic advice to major corporations and his family.

Also by Daniel Petre

The Clever Country? (with David Harrington)
Father and Child
What Matters

FATHER TIME

Daniel Petre

Jane Curry Publishing

This edition published by Jane Curry Publishing
(Wentworth Concepts Pty Ltd T/A) 2005
220a Glenmore Road, Paddington, NSW 2021
First published 1998 by Pan Macmillan Australia

National Library of Australia
Cataloguing-in-publication data:

Petre, Daniel.
Father Time: making time for your children.

Rev. ed.
Bibliography.
ISBN 1 920727 17 5.

1. Father and child. 2. Fatherhood. 3. Work and family.
4. Fatherhood–Psychological aspects. 5. Fathers–Family
relationships. 6. Fathers–Employment. I. Title.

306.8742

Cover and internal design: Liz Seymour
Cover photo: Getty Images
Typeset in 12½/16pt Life by Midland Typesetters
Printed in Australia by McPherson's Printing Group

Contents

Preface

Seven years after the initial publication of *Father Time*, reports on the ability of fathers to play a real part in the lives of their children are mixed. Since 1998 the level of discussion in the media and the workplace about the need for parents to spent time with their children has increased. More flexible work-management practices are being adopted and there is an increasing openness to engage in the debate. This is all very positive. Unfortunately, with few exceptions, our business leaders continue to propagate the notion that to have a successful career you need to sell your soul to the organisation. We continue to have dysfunctional, unbalanced individuals establishing the benchmark for workers.

I am convinced, however, that new fathers today can see more clearly how they want to interact with their children and to what extent they will allow work to control their life. Organisations that want to harness the skills of our best and brightest will have to modify their approach to accommodate the fathers of the twenty-first century.

This book is neither the product of careful research nor the learned view of an expert. It is a product of someone passionately concerned about fathers in society. Because of my career I am particularly concerned at the way senior executives behave both as fathers and as workplace models. Our business leaders have established a value system that, while chasing the reward of profit, has undermined the role fathers need to play in society.

While I have attempted to limit my comments to areas where I have had specific experiences or been able to make observations, I believe much of what I apply here to executive fathers can equally be applied to other fathers as well.

Since launching this book I have received more than 400 letters and emails from fathers and mothers relating their personal struggle to build both a career and a strong bond with their children. What I didn't realise when I wrote *Father Time* is that there is a high level of angst in the parent population. Parents want to have a successful career and they also desperately want to be relevant to their children. They want more understanding and flexibility in their workplaces. They want challenging work roles, but they also want the ability to manage their time so they can invest in both their career and family. I now know the stories and experiences that are the core of *Father Time* are relevant to many fathers.

My daughters are now sixteen, twelve and eight and the intervening eight years have reinforced my belief in the role fathers can and should play in the development of their children. I have now seen first-hand how some fathers allow their obsession for work to take their focus away from their teenage daughter who is struggling to deal with the heightened expectations we place on 'near adults'. I have seen parents try to be their children's best mate and forget that kids need the boundaries a parent creates. Children need their parents to be parents and not their best mates. They need their parents to help them navigate their way through an increasingly complex world and not just push them out the front door on Saturday night with $50 in their pocket and no concern as to what they are doing and where they are going.

I believe the stories and issues that follow are just as relevant today as they were when *Father Time* was initially published. I hope that you find this revised and updated edition relevant, inspiring and maybe just a little life challenging.

Daniel Petre, 2005

Introduction

I first thought of writing a book about my experiences in business and as a father after an interview I gave to the *Sydney Weekly* in 1995. The interview was very different to what I had been used to. Normally the interviewer, usually from a business or computer publication, would want to delve into the strategies and financials underpinning the phenomenon of the information industry.

In this case, however, the interviewer was more interested in finding out what I thought about life, the family, the role of work and many other concepts not connected with work. I found the interview both refreshing and challenging. It was fun to be able to expound my ideas on the purpose of life, but in so doing I had to challenge some of my basic attitudes and motivations.

I also found that I had a deep passion about fathering and yet I had no way of expressing my feelings adequately. I realised as well that I had become somewhat of an observer of society and in particular the behaviour of business fathers. The interview gave me my first opportunity to outline some of my observations and the conclusions I had come to.

I spoke about some of the lessons I had learned about life, especially the importance of balance in life. I also commented on a wide range of other subjects, such as the business culture men have created and the poor management skills in Australian companies, but mainly about being an involved father.

After the interview was published, I received some very interesting feedback. Most of it was favourable, but some was quite negative. I was surprised to find that my strongest critics were all very senior businessmen.

Moreover, they were in careers that were all-encompassing. Their work schedule normally called for twelve-hour days with the more than occasional weekend and late-night session thrown in. Some of them were young executives, men in their early thirties who had done very well in a narrow career sense but had yet to experience life in its fullest form, including marriage, children and the responsibilities they entail. The rest were men aged forty-five or more. While many of this latter group had been married and had children, they seemed to have a very vague idea of the importance of being involved fathers, as well as a very distorted view of the importance of work.

WORK AND FAMILY

My comments were based on my work and family experiences. It seemed clear to me that if you wanted you could try to be a success in your career and also be a great father, spouse and community member. It was all a matter of establishing a balanced approach to your life and also being very clear on what were the *really* important aspects of life.

A key hurdle to overcome was making sure that you were

focused on the truly important areas of life and that you were spending your energy in these areas. Many people would tell me that they felt that the family was the most important part of their life—as they went off to work for sixty-plus hours a week, travelled extensively for work and played golf all day Saturday. Their rhetoric was way out in front of their actions.

But it also had become clear to me that the role of the father has been critically undervalued by society over recent years.

ABOUT MYSELF

I must state at the outset that I do not profess to be a trained psychologist or family therapist. Nor do I have any formal training, if there is such a thing, in terms of being a good parent. Time will tell whether I end up having been a good father and spouse.

I have had a very successful career in the computer industry in three major corporations, followed by a senior role working for one of Australia's largest media companies. I have held leading management positions in both Australia and the U.S., in diverse areas from marketing to software development.

More recently, I have been exposed to the leadership-development industry through consulting work and the not-for-profit sector with the Petre Foundation. Much of what appears in this book comes from my reading and my diverse work experiences.

My career has brought me into close personal contact with business and government leaders in Australia, the U.S. and Asia. I have been able to see at first hand how many of our leading companies operate and also gain some understanding of how the senior managers in these companies view the issues of work-family balance and the role of the father. My disappointment at what I have observed convinced me of the need to communicate my concerns at some very disturbing trends I see emerging in our society.

SEEING THE LIGHT

I did not always think as I do now. I was a classic fast-track, hard-nosed workaholic. Then one day I woke up and realised that my life was out of balance. I suddenly decided that working seventy-hour weeks in the pursuit of greater market share and financial success for my employer was really not the most important thing in my life. This is not to say that work is not a key motivator as regards both self-esteem and monetary reward. Work not only enables people to satisfy their material needs, but often provides them with a network of friends, as well as the opportunity to express themselves creatively in an area they find interesting. Having acknowledged this, it is important to return to the point that work should not take over a person's life.

I came to the realisation that balance in life was the key to the health and wellbeing of my family and myself. I believed I could obtain balance in my life by making concessions without having to necessarily trade off any career success to obtain fulfilment in other aspects of my life. While working through the balance issue, I also became concerned that fathers no longer seemed to be considered a vital part of a child's development. It was accepted to find fathers of the 1950s generation conforming to the remote model that was promoted when they were married, but I was distressed to find that a lot of younger men were approaching fatherhood the same way. At the same time society appeared to be saying that apart from their role as impregnators and income-earners fathers were not required. We seem to have reached the point where fathers are beginning to feel that to be "better men" they need to work longer hours and not necessarily spend more time with their children. The father of today thinks he is doing a good job because of what he materially provides for his children. He does not realise that, once his children are fed and housed, being a father has a lot more to do with time.

KIDS IN CARE

Society has made significant progress with regard to a woman's right to live a life with as much choice as a man. With the fight for equality having nearly turned the corner, women are now taking up more important leadership roles in business and government. The increased earning capacity of professional women has meant they can take care of their families even if their marriages have dissolved. This increased autonomy for at least some women has brought many positive results. Girls can now grow up confident of being able to choose virtually any career on increasingly equal terms with boys. As the father of three girls I am very pleased that through the struggle of others my daughters will have more opportunities in their lives than generations of women in the past. While opportunities for women have grown, society still maintains an expectation that the mother is responsible for the day to day childrearing. Men have not assumed a more equal role in terms of the daily care of the children.

However, the increase in women's participation in the workforce has meant that more and more children are growing up under the primary supervision of childcare workers, both during the day and after school. There has not been a noticeable increase in fathers staying at home to look after their children while their mother goes off to work. The range of child care options has grown from the traditional model of the mother taking care of the child to the mother taking care of the child by placing it in day care. In reality the mother does not get the same choice as the father (whether to take care of the child, or work and have the child looked after by their spouse, or have the child looked after by some form of day care facility). Many parents believe that the combination of the stimulation of daycare and the 'quality' time spent with parents at some point during the week is a wonderful environment for their children. So we have developed a society which suggests that outside care is an appropriate alternative to parental care (in fact some will even say it is better for children). But what of men? Men seem to be working longer hours.

In recent times the working week has steadily grown longer for many people. In particular, the average number of hours worked by male office workers has increased significantly over the last twenty years. So what is the problem?

Two Men. Two very different lives

Two men's lives illustrate opposite ends of the executive father spectrum. Both were men with whom I worked in the early years of my career and it is only over more recent times, since becoming a father, that I have been able to look back on their experiences with some degree of understanding.

One man, John, was a senior marketing executive in a large computer company. He is a very warm, friendly and caring man. He got married and then had children in his late thirties. The arrival of his children coincided with a dramatic increase in the demands of his job. He was a stellar success in what was a very frenetic work environment. Lots of travel, major product releases, tremendous coverage in the media, new campaigns—an exciting time. The work day started before 8 a.m. and rarely finished before 7.30 p.m. The combination of his long work day and level of travel meant that he was not home a lot during these years.

He was happy, successful and an all-round great guy. He was very attentive to his wife and made sure that she shared in the fruits of his labour: huge bonuses and lots of incentive trips.

I left the company and lost contact with him for some years. When he did meet up again things had changed somewhat for him, as he had also left the company and started up his own marketing organisation.

Over lunch one day he started not by talking about how his career had changed and how much he missed the overseas travel, large expensive accounts and corporate boxes at the rugby, but how lucky he was in that his change of career had made him take greater notice of his relationship with his children. He explained that in his rush to succeed he had missed the first six years of his children's lives and now that he spent more time with them he realised he didn't really know them well.

His story has a happy ending. He started to focus on spending more time with his children. He developed a very strong relationship with both of his kids that endures today. His new marketing company went on to become very successful and yet he never returned to the very long work days and remote father-child relationship of his previous job.

Even today he talks with a lot of passion about how close he came to never really knowing his children and that if he had stayed to his original course he would have ended up being not only a poor father but a very unhappy one as well.

And then there was Barry. He was a general manager for a company that worked closely with the company I was working for. Barry was a classic entrepreneur. He was very bright, personable, creative and energetic. He had been married twice and with his second wife he had fathered three children. At the time that I got to know him, his children's ages were between six and ten. He had always worked very hard, having built up two major companies over the previous decade.

Over the five years that I knew him he maintained a very focused attitude to work. All meetings were critical ones. Every deal had to be won. There was never enough time to do all the business deals that he wanted to do. Every year he would take his sales team on lavish incentive trips to exotic locations. Wives included; children excluded. While I was not yet married and had no concept of the trade-offs of having children, I noticed that he seemed to talk a lot about his kids and I assumed he must be really involved with them.

As happened with John, I lost contact with Barry. On returning to Australia some seven years after leaving my employer at the time, I met Barry and found out what had happened to him in that time. I guess with wisdom it was not surprising. His business suffered some major problems during the early 1990s requiring even more focus and commitment of energy. He separated from his wife but they did eventually get back together.

When I caught up with him in 1993 I asked him about his children. He explained that he didn't see much of them. He started to explain that it was good that his children were living independent lives and that they didn't need him around. It was right and proper that children grow up and take responsibility for their own lives. Of course he would like to see them more but he understood that they were very busy. Midway through his explanation I noticed a profound sadness come across his face. He stopped mid sentence and pondered: 'If I had known this was how it was going to end up with my kids I would have lived a very different life'. I felt incredibly sorry for him. Of course he could still try to develop a relationship with his children but both he and I knew that it was very hard road given what had occurred during their growing years.

Two men. Similar environments and similar early career experiences. One, through luck or design, had been given the opportunity to stop for a brief moment and see clearly where his life was heading and how far away from his children he really was. The other had remained caught up in his world of work and only saw the result of this unbalanced approach after it was arguably too late to have a material effect.

DADDY, WE HARDLY KNOW YOU

The fundamental problem is that many children lack any significant level of fathering in their lives. Our society has neglected the role of the father and failed to recognise the important part the father-child relationship plays in the development of both the father and the child.

While I don't believe that even the most wonderful childcare worker (and there are many who are truly wonderful people) can really take the role of the child's mother, I can accept that as most childcare workers are women, children in their charge will develop a good understanding of child-female relationships. But how do they develop an understanding of child-male relationships?

This can't be expected to take place during the few minutes a day the average male executive spends with his children. Perhaps even more worrying then are those children who, through the breakdown of their parents' marriage, rarely interact with their father at all.

As a society we don't seem to acknowledge or care that our children are growing up fatherless.

Macho Man and Bully Managers

As mentioned earlier, some people found my emphasis on a search for balance and a greater role for fathers refreshing and yet strange. Strange in that someone who had a very successful career and who was still less than forty years old was questioning the concept of work obsession and the macho ethic of most Australian companies, and most importantly challenged people to make their families the major priority in their lives.

My earlier experiences had made me think that to be successful I would have to emulate the 'bully' managers who seemed to dominate Australian companies. Business magazines were (and still are) full of hero-worship stories about 'hard-nosed' executives who had taken the 'hard line' and through their obsessive approach lifted a business out of a loss situation into significant profit. We are often presented with 'business icons' who have created immense wealth for shareholders or turned around commercial disasters. We rarely gain an understanding of what sort of a manager such people are or what sort of parent, spouse or friend they are.

We are told that business success is the definition of success and that to be a success you should strive to make money. It seemed strange to me then, as it does now, that intelligent multi-skilled human beings could be so simplistic in terms of evaluating the work and life of an individual.

Often these heroes had discarded their responsibilities to their children and spouses; they had brought to many companies a culture of fear and intimidation and work obsession. Sure, the companies made a book profit but did anyone measure the real cost of these 'heroes'' effort?

I have worked for managers in the past (thankfully many years ago) who fit the mould of the 'bully' manager. While exhibiting all the ugly attributes described above I also found these men to be, in nearly all cases, lonely, lost men who lacked confidence in dealing with people on equal terms. Their insecurity

> led them to use their power and role to define their
> environment.
>   Thus while disliking their approach to managing
> people, I also felt very sorry for them.

LONG HOURS ARE WRONG HOURS

One of the issues we have to deal with is the idea that long
hours on the job is a good thing. If there is a consistent
thread running through this book it is that long work hours
are bad. People who get sucked into believing they have to
work long hours to be successful are undermining their
ability to develop a strong relationship with their children,
and without a father around their children have a greater
chance of getting into trouble.

Generally we are led to believe that a forty-hour week is
reasonable, from both an economic and a human point of
view. Yet, especially in white-collar jobs, people are often
working fifty-, sixty- or even seventy-hour weeks. The
problem is partly due to the fact that in many offices the
job is never done and the tasks at hand can take widely
differing amounts of time. As a result, we have created a
work ethic where people regularly put in absurdly long
hours. Some social wombats may elect to have no life
outside of work, but unfortunately these kinds of hours are
now seen as the 'norm' in most white-collar environments
and people who do not work the same hours are seen as
lazy or, at worst, not dedicated to their careers.

This so-called ethic has pervaded all our professions and
most other white-collar work. There is never any serious
debate about the detrimental effects on the individual's

health, let alone his or her family life, by promoting such hours as the accepted level of commitment. Nor is there any discussion of the relationship between excessive hours and productivity. Surely if an employee is tired from over-work, the law of diminishing returns begins to operate.

Yet the final outcome is not just diminishing returns but ultimately a shorter life. There exists significant research in the U.S. and the U.K. that very long work hours lead to an increase in health risks for employees. Increased levels of heart disease, cancer and stress-related sicknesses are found in people who consistently work very long hours.

A small insight into this process occurs when hard-working people take a holiday. I know many people, including myself, who have worked long days for weeks (or months) and then take a holiday. The pattern seems to be that you spend the first few days on holiday suffering from stress-related sicknesses. It is as though when your body notices it has an opportunity for a break it basically breaks down. You seem to catch colds and other viruses very easily and then take some of your holiday break to recover.

Are we surprised that a continual diet of long work days leaves a legacy of major health issues?

WORK HARD—INVEST WHEN IT MATTERS

As a manager in an industry that is regarded as being very fast-paced and very challenging I constantly reminded my employees that, other than in extreme emergency situa-tions, I did not expect them to work more than an average of forty-five hours a week. (Of course this is more than the 37.5 hours under most standard awards, but this extra effort is required in our industry.) I also told them that I didn't want them at work at night and I didn't want them at work on weekends. I believe that if you are working much more than forty-five hours a week regularly you are not looking after your health, you are not being a responsible parent and you are probably a lousy partner.

The balance is that when you are at work you are expected to work hard. Come to work, work hard and then go home and make sure the rest of your life is getting some focus.

I have been ridiculed in many quarters for my approach to time mangement. Unfortunately for my detractors, in each role I have held the performance of my group using any quantifiable measure has always been well above expectations.

PROFIT FOR PROFIT'S SAKE

Some time ago a good friend of mine, Jack Heath, introduced me to Steve Biddulph's book, *Manhood*. As I read the book I began to realise that the thoughts I had been formulating were not as random as I had suspected. I realised that I was lucky enough to have woken up from the comatose state of work obsession and had done so in time to ensure I could develop a deep and long-term relationship with my kids, my wife and my inner self.

Most importantly, I have started to realise that through the last fifty or so years we (men) have created business infrastructures that are basically anti-children, anti-family, anti-spouse, anti-community and anti-anything approaching social responsibility. These infrastructures are pro-profit. This is seen as the ultimate excuse. It is as though making a profit absolves us of all sins and justifies any practice, however harmful:

- It doesn't matter that some of our companies promote and sell products that while legal, affect our children's long-term health.
- It doesn't matter that the pollution from our factory is killing our rivers because we make a profit.
- It doesn't matter that some media companies bias the news in a way that plays up the bad aspects of our society, thus fuelling human fear, because we make a profit.
- It doesn't matter that we build environmentally inappropriate buildings and structures because we make a profit.

Profit is a measure of the financial performance of a company. It in no way measures whether the company is conducting business in a way that assists the social development of its workforce or its customer base. Profit doesn't measure the physical and mental stress placed on employees and their families. It doesn't measure the effect of political infighting rampant in most Australian corporations. Profit doesn't give any indication of the long-term positioning of our country. Profit is in many ways a trick.

The trick is that we convince ourselves that if we are profitable then we are OK. The guy with the biggest profit is the best, no matter how questionable his behaviour might be.

Manhood and Executives

Steve Biddulph, whose book *Manhood* has reached a quarter of a million Australians with its positive message about men and change, has a more charitable view. He calls it a practice effect. Men like and need to feel competent, and this is a very positive side to our character. But in fatherhood, in the messy business of home life, we often feel like complete idiots. We haven't got experience of how to be with kids, and it seems overwhelming. If our partner is even half competent, the temptation to leave it to her is very strong.

After all, the calmer, more organised workplace is where we have built up our skills and defences. The tragedy of this is that if we don't get that early learning in, and grow comfortable with the company of our children when they are still young and need us, then we may simply never be at ease with them. Millions of white-collar men have suffered this fate in the last three generations. They become distant through working too hard in the years when their children are babies, often through quite real financial pressures, and by the time they want to know their teenage or adult children, it seems too hard because the foundations aren't there.

Steve believes that fathers can build up a kind of experience-equity by sharing experiences with children, for instance through travelling together, and by having activities they carry out one-to-one with each child. From the age of two, fathers can take 'total care weekends' where their partner has a night or two away and leaves them to it! It's a simple matter of being willing to enter a new learning curve, where you may feel like a klutz for a while, but rapidly gain your own confidence to be able to manage, cook for, clean, and enjoy children and teenagers in the ways that only fathers really can.

One tip Steve offers is to avoid the 'theme park—junk food—stack of videos' syndrome, which can leave your spirit as well as your wallet feeling empty and used. Kids already just see their corporate dad as a walking credit card. It's better to actually do things with your children. Get into nature (in manageable chunks!). Do it with another father friend if you need moral support. Be prepared to have the odd fight or showdown with kids, who aren't always sure how to be around you, any more than you are with them. You get closer through fighting, as well as through having good times. Just keep your sense of humour, and don't give up when it gets a little tense. You are laying down lifetime memories, every single day or weekend you spend cements the connections which will be there for life.

WHAT'S THE REAL WORTH?

I think it would be better if we looked at companies in terms of the net result of their activities for individuals and for society as a whole. Suppose we have two companies— one that exhibits all that is wrong with business practices as described above and one that exhibits a more enlightened view of the world in terms of respect for the environment, the quality of its products, the wellbeing of its employees, and so on. But what if the first company is ten per cent more profitable than the second? How should we measure the real worth of these companies?

Unfortunately our financial markets will always vote for the first company. Yet by any reasonable standard the second company is providing more value to society and to the country.

Apart from its greater sense of social responsibility, its employees are less stressed, thus making fewer demands on the health system. They have deeper and more sustainable relationships with their families, thus perhaps reducing marital breakdown and potential problems with their children. Surely the total cost to society of Company 2 is much less than that of Company 1, and yet the profit measure lets Company 1 win every time.

TAKING A NEW DIRECTION

This book is not about trying to change the way financial markets measure companies as the concept is a very complex one and perhaps profit is the best practical yardstick they can use (from a bad set of choices). This book is not so ambitious as to attempt—overnight—to change the work hour regime in Australia. It has a more gradual, subversive aim of encouraging common sense to prevail in those individuals who are open to new ways of thinking, or sick of the old way of life. The aim of the book is to achieve a dual goal—companies that are productive *and* successful, by the very fact that their staff, from CEO to cleaners, are happier and more well-adjusted people. Family-friendly companies, which are also investor-friendly and socially responsible—this *has* to be the way of the future.

One of the goals of this book is to help men and their friends, spouses and children really think about what they are doing with their lives and the direction their lives are taking. Specifically I hope it makes at least a few work-obsessed fathers stop and see what is happening to themselves and their families before it is too late. If only a few fathers take stock of things and make the appropriate changes then this book will have served its purpose.

I also want to appeal to our chief executives. There is no question that senior managers set the tone and culture of their companies. In my opinion they have to realise that in many cases they have been responsible for establishing structures that are anti-family and very much anti-father. The long-term benefit of a change towards family-friendly companies will be profound. Those to make these changes will be the survivors and innovators of tomorrow, because they will attract the best staff, inspire the most loyalty, and have real energy and an esprit de corps.

CHANGING THE BUSINESS ENVIRONMENT

In many ways perhaps the main goal of this book is to help men in the corporate world see the problems with the environment they have created and help recraft a new one.

Because of its reliance on the profit motive and its emphasis on 'hours worked', the business environment often has some extremely anti-social and even anti-human features. Chief among these is the way in which it is undermining the role of the father. It also burdens society with very heavy costs as a result of the loss of fathering.

I believe that if men start to adopt more open and caring attitudes, then we will see a shift in how companies and governments operate. We will have created a momentum for change that will involve not only men but the whole community and the net benefit to society will be immense.

There will be casualties along the way as these changes gather pace. Men who have based their lives on work obsession—let alone managing through fear, intimidation and raw power—will find themselves out of step and isolated. People will not want to work in their companies and customers will no longer buy their products. Their families and friends will tend to shun them as they become disenchanted with such men's approach to family and personal relationships.

Men who see the need to change and allow themselves to be more human will start to experience a depth in personal relationships that they have never had before. They will begin to see a long-term purpose in their lives, they will develop closer friendships and they will create environments that people want to work within.

SPEAKING PERSONALLY

The following chapters are based on events that have shaped my life or what I consider to be major aspects of the role of the father in society. I am in my forties and am still learning about life, but I know I have built myself a strong and resilient base, capable of coping with the forces at work in society. I know that I am creating a space around me that allows me to develop deep relationships with my friends and family and to work with people who are happy, motivated and in control of themselves.

I know that I will continue to have a successful career and yet I will do this while keeping my family as my main priority and ensuring my life is a balanced one. If nothing else I want to use this book as a way of saying that in life you can have it all, as long as you are prepared to make some concessions and remain committed to your long-term goals.

BEFORE WE REALLY GET STARTED ...

When I talk of a family I mean the group of people, relatives and others whom you hold dear to your heart and to whom you feel a responsibility to help protect and nurture. A family can be made up of your spouse and children or of your lover and close friends. It includes all those you consider very close to you and whom you would say you love very much.

Similarly, I do not look at fathering as purely the process of creating a child through the fertilisation of an egg. Rather I see it as a process whereby men use their natural and developed skills to nurture, love, educate and protect. Thus fathering can be undertaken by men in relation to their sons and daughters, other young men and women, friends, or even organisations.

Fathering is a skill that needs to be both celebrated and acknowledged. With more good fathering we could truly have a better world for all.

1
Lost fathers

We are within a generation of losing forever a sense of what fathering is all about. A plastic shell-like doll, made for TV and economically sleek, is replacing the fully-rounded figure of the nurturing and protecting father in traditional society. This is the ultimate form of a model which first took shape at the time of the Industrial Revolution. It is inherently corrupt and is destroying our families and our lives.

THE DISTANT RELATION

While men continue to produce children physically, increasingly the father is becoming a distant family relation. An increase in work hours for much of the population has meant that fathers are less often at home. Moreover, when they are at home their children are asleep or the fathers are still in work-mode, finishing off some leftover office task. Less time is being spent by fathers not only sharing their knowledge of life but more importantly helping their children's emotional development.

It's true that many men also play a fatherly role for

childen who are not their own. Men who coach sporting teams and male teachers often provide children, especially boys, with the male bonding that is so important to a child's development. But there are generally fewer parents involved in community activities with children than there were some years ago.

MANLESS CLASSROOM

The teaching profession is also rapidly losing its male members. The fact that society so undervalues the group of people who, apart from parents, have the most significant influence on future generations defies logic. Many Asian countries which believe, as we claim to do, that children represent the future actually put their resources behind education. Funding is seen as a high priority and not an area for constant reduction. But in Australia the poor financial rewards mean that in public schools we have fewer men teachers than women and their numbers are constantly declining.

While teachers, whether male or female, have an equally significant influence on the development of the young, children must be given the opportunity to build healthy relationships with adults of both sexes on a regular basis. This is as important at school, where they spend most of their day, as at home. Of course this does not mean that thrusting children into random situations with adults is at all healthy. What is required is an environment where stable, healthy relationships can develop between them.

WRONG ROLE-MODELS

Together with the fact that men as fathers or surrogate fathers are spending much less time with children than they should is the increasing emphasis on materialism in its ugliest form. Newspapers are full of 'heroes' whose only achievement has been to make money. Little attention is paid to how they accumulated their wealth, whether their business practices are ethical and moral, whether they are good family men, or whether they have done anything for the community. Money has become the balm with which the popular press anoints its idols. We have lost the ability to see people as real human beings with both good and bad points or judge them on the depth of their character.

The elevation of such dubious types to star status gives us very poor role-models to follow. Some people who are sufficiently strong-willed and independent to keep their attitudes and values intact will be able to find their own way through these confusing influences. The rest of us, however, do look for someone who can act as an example to help guide us through life. Unfortunately the media do not take their responsibilities seriously enough and keep coming up with false models for us to emulate, based only on the measure of financial success.

WHOM DO I TURN TO?

So where does a new father turn to learn the skills he is going to need? As a soon-to-be-father in 1989 I wandered into a large city bookstore in search of some books that could help prepare me for what I was about to be thrown into. I found a fair range of books dealing with a baby's development and the mother's physical and emotional development both before and after giving birth. There were very few books which even acknowledged that the father had a role to play. A couple were semi-humorous, introducing fathers to the pleasures of baby vomit, midnight screaming and baby diarrhoea. But there was nothing to help me understand better what I should be doing, and how I should be dealing with my own thoughts and emotions.

Attending 'baby classes' reinforced this impression. While it was acknowledged that the father had some role to play—mainly limited to impregnation and assisting his wife during labour—nobody seemed to be interested in supporting him as an active, informed participant in his child's development. The Department of Health organises 'playgroups' to allow new mothers to meet up and share their experiences of child-bearing. But there were no forums where fathers could engage in any detailed discussion about the arrival of their child and what it meant to them. This of course continued a long tradition of men dealing in silence with major events in their lives, so it was probably not surprising to find such a lack of services for the father.

The result is that the father who wants to find out more about his new role becomes quickly discouraged. He goes back to being the uninformed support-assistant to his wife—as though he has no other function than that of support. Of course, supporting your wife is a key role and one that most fathers accept as an important task, though there is always the odd exception. I recall one senior executive at Microsoft who used to boast about his dedication to the company by telling people that he was away on business for the birth of all three of his children. Perhaps he will wake up one day and realise he has missed one of life's most magical and important moments (three times!!) for the sake of better revenue performance. A high price to pay.

PASSIVE FATHERHOOD

Restricting the father's role to support undervalues the part he can and should play in the birth and development of a child. It also presupposes that fathers have either little interest in what is happening or little of value to add. One could be excused for thinking that fathering is nothing more than a biological process. Many fathers' personal involvement with their children is prescribed by a tight agenda drawn up by their wives, almost like a manual on how to be a dad until mum gets home. The common attitude that mothers should provide explicit instructions needs to be reviewed. Is it that men are genetically incompetent when it comes to looking after children or that they do not have the interest? Part of the problem lies in what society has accepted as normal behaviour. This has resulted in a pattern that has become perpetuated.

In a study some years ago E.R. Goldsmith and J.H. Greenhaus* looked at differing models of work and family. They reported on earlier research by Joseph Pleck which suggested that social norms 'permit' women to forego work activities in the face of family responsibilities, whereas men are permitted to forego family activities in favour of work commitments. Fathers now use part of the time they would once have spent with their families to go to work, just as

* For this and other works cited, see the References at the end of the book.

it has been considered normal practice for women to give up work to have children. The establishment of social norms that put a father's work ahead of his family responsibilities creates a false sense of what society needs from fathers.

FACTORIES AND FATHERING

The effect of the Industrial Revolution on fatherhood has been well documented by many writers, including Steve Biddulph in *Manhood* and Adrienne Burgess in *Fatherhood Reclaimed*. In the second half of the 19th century as industrialisation intensified, fathers increasingly left the traditional home environment to work in the new factories. The family structure changed dramatically. The father was now no longer at home during the day and thus children missed out on the importance of his influence during their growing years. According to Burgess, early 20th century family experts declared that this new form of part-time fathering was actually desirable, somehow allowing a weary father to return home from the day's work with a fresh approach to issues in the family domain.

The detached father who was created during the Industrial Revolution and still exists today was a new phenomenon. Previously, as many accounts of the time make clear, fathers would show a great deal of public affection for their children, nursing their babies and playing with them whenever they could.

Paedophile Paranoia

Many of the historical structures that supported the fathering process are disappearing. Fathers are now less seen as the protectors of children—even less so, perhaps, following the report of the Wood Royal Commissions in NSW into paedophilia. I know of many men who work in schools and other environments with children and who are now almost paranoid about the possible misinterpretation of their motives. It is important to ensure that children are protected and that child abuse in our schools is never again tolerated. Unfortunately, as with any issue arousing such strong community concern, many men have tended to overreact. We must not allow a situation to develop where men are not able to act in a normal, healthy and acceptable way with children that they are in contact with.

Recently a friend of mine was at his child's school playing a game of chasing with the youngsters. The child or parent who was 'in' would chase the other kids, catch and tickle one of them and then the captured group would chase the 'free' kids until all were caught. The kids loved having a parent involved. At one point my friend was 'in' and he caught and tickled a child, as was part of the game. Afterwards another parent who was watching came up and said that she felt it was perhaps not a good idea to catch and tickle kids, given the current climate with regard to paedophiles. My friend was devastated and has since avoided playing such games at school any more. Did he overreact? Perhaps, but it's hard to imagine any adult wanting school gossip suggesting that his actions are anything but those of an involved and loving parent.

There is a danger that in our eagerness to expose the

> depraved individuals who prey on children we will end
> up persecuting the innocent. We must weed out the
> undesirable elements while encouraging more men to
> express their warmth and love of children.

DUAL PROVIDERS

Men are no longer the sole providers of resources for the
family. While this is a generally positive trend, it nonetheless removes what has been for centuries a major characteristic underpinning the role of the father. It needs to be
replaced with something that men can identify with in
defining their role.

As a result of the increased participation of women in
the workforce, the provider role is now split and the father
is no longer the major influence on the formation of a
child's view of the outside world. The fact that the mother
is now as significant an influence is again a very healthy
development, in that it ensures that children gain the
benefit of at least two major sources of influence in their
early years. As they grow older the number of possible
influences on them grows and the role of both parents
declines, particularly that of the father. Hence the father's
position in the family needs to be redefined in a clear way,
giving a positive lead on what his responsibilities now are.

Historically fathers have provided a strong developmen-
tal role with regard to their children's work. In the second
half of the 19th century in the U.K. more than fifty per
cent of children entered their father's trade.

Clearly the children were being trained into particular

trades or professions by their fathers; long hours were spent ensuring the child picked up the skill that would allow him to become employable in his father's trade.

Yet with this concentration of time spent with their fathers these children were also learning skills other than those focused on a particular trade. Fathers were able to impart life lessons to their children and children were able to develop very strong relationships with their father.

While the trend away from 'following in your father's footsteps' is healthy for many reasons—not the least allowing a child to develop a truly independent life mapped by their own interests—we also lost this sense of a father providing 'life education' to their children. It is the loss of this second level of education that is problematic for today's society.

SYMBOLIC FATHERS

One of the most negative attitudes towards fatherhood I have come across was that of the early child psychologist D.W. Winnicott, who followed the popular view of his day that the father was really most important as a symbol. His role was to 'turn up often enough for the child to feel he was real and alive'. So much for any concept of involved fathering.

In discussions with executive groups I have heard a similar view expressed. Many executive fathers say explicitly they believe it is both right and proper for the children not to see a lot of their father. Comments such as 'leaving them to their own devices builds self-esteem and individuality' are common, ignoring the fact that all research on the subject indicates that such outcomes are not the result of leaving kids alone.

Too often fathers look at their responsibilities purely in the light of their own experiences. Such views are irrational, given the changes that have occurred in society over the last forty years. Harking back to a frequently faulty memory of one's own childhood is no help in coping with the problems of fathering today. Some men argue that because they were brought up by their fathers in a particular way and turned out well, their children will do likewise with the same treatment. This is like saying, 'When I was young my father used to beat me with a cricket bat and I survived, therefore I can beat my kids.' The fact that some children whose fathers spent little time with them, showed them no emotion or physically abused them grew up with no apparent emotional scars does not mean that such neglect was right.

One father I know, who is a real workaholic and is rarely home in time to see his children, defends his approach by using this logic. 'My father used to work long hours and I never saw him and yet I turned out all right, so I think my kids will too.' This sounds more like a shallow justification of his obsession with work than a well thought-out decision on what is best for his kids. What should be done is to combine the positive aspects of your past with some firm ideas of your own on what good fathering should be about.

ALL ON THEIR OWN

The effect of children spending time alone must be taken into account. In the book *The Time Bind*, A.R. Hochschild quotes a study of nearly five thousand eighth-graders in the

U.S. and their parents which found that children who were home alone for eleven or more hours a week were three times more likely than other youngsters to abuse alcohol, tobacco or marijuana. This was true for both upper-class and working-class children. Research on adults who had been left home alone as children suggested that they ran a far higher risk of developing 'substantial fear responses'— recurring nightmares, fear of noise, fear of the dark and fear for their personal safety. Hochschild states:

In the grip of a time bind, working parents redefine as nonessential more than a child's need for security and companionship. The blockbuster film, Home Alone, *in which a child left by himself emerges as a heroic everyboy, masks the anxiety that infuses the subject of children home alone with upbeat denial. One husband in Amerco commented, 'We don't really need a hot meal at night because we eat well at lunch.' A mother wondered why she should bother to cook beans for her children when her son didn't like them. Yet another challenged the need for children's daily baths or clean clothes: 'He loves his brown pants. Why shouldn't he just wear them for a week?' Of a three-month-old child in nine-hour daycare a father assured me, 'I want him to be independent.'*

In the study of the giant Amerco firm in 1990 to which Hochschild refers (although the name was changed in the book to protect the company), it was found that twenty-seven per cent of children between the ages of six and thirteen stayed home alone while both parents were at work. Of course twelve-year-olds can look after themselves physically when they get home from school, but like all children they basically need to share their experiences and talk about their problems during the day. By the time 6 or 7 p.m. comes around children no longer have the sense of urgency to discuss their problems or, perhaps more seriously, they have internalised the problems as a result of having no outlet.

Latchkey Children

A friend of mine was a latchkey child from the age of ten. His parents had to work as only with a combined income could the family have a reasonable lifestyle. He was quite capable at an early age of cooking, cleaning and generally taking care of himself. But for a couple of years his afternoon regime was less than pleasant. He used to walk home and unfortunately there was a group of four or five older boys he would encounter on the way. Although he was quite a tall and strong boy he was no match for them and most afternoons he would try to get out of class early and race home before they caught up with him or wait back in the hope that they had gone ahead. I only became aware of his situation years later when he told me how he would often get to his front door, with the 'pack' in pursuit, only to fumble with the key. Sometimes he got inside before they arrived, sometimes not. Even when he was 'caught' nothing terribly bad happened—just normal adolescent bullying like pushing him around and kicking his school case. But the emotional damage they caused him was considerable.

When I asked him why he didn't tell anyone he said that at the time he felt that he would have been branded a 'wimp' if he had informed his teachers or his parents or even his friends. I felt incredibly sorry for him, that he would put up with this routine every afternoon for fear of being called a coward.

I also vividly recall a female friend who was infatuated with another friend of mine but whose love was not returned. One afternoon, as she and her schoolmates were waiting for their buses home, another girl announced that she was 'going around' with my male friend. The jilted girl friend burst into tears and ran off. Some hours later, she rang me to talk about this tragedy in her life. It is easy now to say that it was just teenage love, but that does not take into account the intensity of her feelings at the time and how hurt she was. When we were talking it was clear that she felt really alone. Both her parents worked and she was an only child. By the time her parents got home she had recovered from her initial distress and I am still not sure whether her mother and father—who were very caring and loving people—knew what happened that day. I can't help but think that she would have coped so much better if she had been able to run home into the arms of one of her parents, someone who could console her and comfort her.

Should a parent be at home in the off-chance that their children will encounter similar situations? Of course not, but equally the examples above indicate what even young people of presumably 'independent' age have to deal with by themselves when growing up as latchkey children. While the opportunity to work has emancipated married women from domestic tyranny, society has not satisfactorily addressed the gap that is now left in our children's lives.

SURROGATE SERVICES

In the past the mother was around not only to provide the services required after school but offer the love, affection and understanding which is difficult for even the most dedicated childcare worker to give. Services abound to help both parents maintain their careers and also have their children's needs attended to. In America, for instance, Hochschild refers to 'Kids in Motion' in Chicago which provides transport to take kids from school to sport or music. 'Playground Connections' in Washington DC matches 'playmates' to one another. In several U.S. cities children call a 1-900 number to contact 'Grandma Please'. There they can make contact with an adult who has time to talk to them, sing to them, listen to their problems, help them with their homework or just make them feel wanted. 'Creative Memories' puts family photos in albums, along with descriptive captions.

These services are a poor substitute for real parent-child interaction. What is lost in this business-like approach is any understanding of a child's feelings and emotions or the role such activities play in providing an opportunity for parents and children to communicate. Taking children to after-school sport is not merely a taxi service. As well as enabling them to talk about the day's events with the parent concerned on the way to the venue, it forces the parent out of the work environment. A father who no longer has to leave work by 5 p.m. to take his son to football because he knows someone else will make sure Johnny gets to the oval on time is unlikely to leave work at 5 p.m. to watch Johnny train.

Increasingly the father is not required to be part of the daily running of his children's lives. He is also seen as non-essential from a 'provision of service' point of view. Nobody seems to care about the child's, or father's, need for the love and bond that they can share.

PARENTS BUT NOT CITIZENS

Parental involvement in their children's lives is diminishing, along with allied social responsibilities. According to the Harvard political scientist Robert Putnam, as quoted by Hochschild, the proportion of Americans reporting that they had attended a public meeting on town or school affairs in the previous year fell from twenty-two per cent in 1973 to thirteen per cent in 1993. Membership in organisations such as the Red Cross, Boy Scouts and Lions Clubs has fallen as well. A similar pattern is also discernible in Australia.

At my eldest daughter's school there are over 1,100 students. That would suggest there would perhaps be around 800 sets of parents (allowing for members of the same family being at school and for single-parent households). Parents' and Citizens' Association (P&C) meetings, where major issues about the school and its plans are discussed, are regularly attended by fewer than fifty people. Unfortunately it is roughly the same fifty people who organise the major events within the school. It is not that the only parents who care for their children are those who attend the meetings but work pressures mean that it is easy to assume 'the school will run by itself'.

One mother who had a son at the local public school moved him to a private school in Year Two. She told me that she intended to become involved in activities at the new school even though she had shown no interest in helping out at the public school. When I asked her the reasons for the change of heart, she told me the parent group at the private school offered both her son and her husband opportunities to create relationships which would be of use during their lives. Her motivation was not so much to help the school but to further her own social ambitions.

MISSING MOTHERS

The problems resulting from children being left alone are clearly not wholly brought about by fathers being focused on work ahead of their families but also by the greater part women now play in the wider community. The fact that stay-at-home mothers have been able to keep the family together in the past does not mean that they should be 'motivated' out of the workforce as some politicians would prefer. What it does suggest is that for quite some time we have lived with an unbalanced home environment, which has only held together because women were at home. As we have seen, the underlying problem of fathers not being involved has been with us for the last couple of centuries. Many fathers also regard providing the money to run the household as a testament to their love and commitment. But as will later be discussed, this is more often an excuse for not spending the time and energy which is really required for good fathering.

FATHER TIME PAYS OFF ...

There is a strong correlation between the time a father spends with a child and the latter's development. As Burgess notes:

Right through adolescence and in many different ways, the benefits to children of positive and substantial father involvement can be measured; in self-control, life skills, and social competence. Adolescents who have good relationships with their fathers take their responsibilities seriously, are more likely to do what their parents ask and are less limited by traditional sex-role expectations. The boys have fewer behavioural problems in school, and the girls are more self-directed, cheerful and happy, willing to try new things. Among adults, both men and women, the strongest predictor of empathetic concern for others is high level of caretaking by their fathers when they were little. Father involvement is also one of the major predictors of whether adults in their twenties will have progressed, educationally and socially, beyond their parents.

Research has repeatedly found that when fathers spend committed time with their children, the benefits are enormous. Among seven- to eleven-year-olds receiving such attention, for instance, there is a much lower incidence of delinquent behaviour, while older children are more likely to go on to higher education and generally have higher career aspirations. Yet all the evidence points to less time being spent between fathers and children.

MEET SOME MODERN DADS

1. VISITATION FATHERS

With more common marital separation and divorce, many fathers have to obey strict conditions of access to their children. I have seen first-hand where what starts as a formalised process of visitation by the father deteriorates over time. Visits become very awkward, with the father knowing he has only a short time available and yet he can't just drop back into his children's lives. He desperately wants to make the time with his kids 'special', but the reality is that it's difficult to thaw out relationships that are lived by a stopwatch. Children who spend most of their lives with their mother are unlikely to want to repeat all last week's experiences so as to update dad—not because they don't love him but because children are not ones to sit back and ponder the past. The 'visitation' father can't help but feel an outsider in his children's lives. The children in turn feel awkward as they are shuttled back and forth and their routine is disrupted, so that such sessions become tense encounters which nobody enjoys. Gradually the father fails to take up his visitation rights and focuses sadly on a new life, unable to rebuild the old one. The slow undermining of the father-child relationship by divorce does not excuse those fathers who fail to meet their financial commitments to their children. Whether or not they can have a relationship with their children, they still have a duty to support them.

Not all divorce situations end up like this. There are many examples of single parents going on to have better lives with their children than would have been possible while they were married. There are also situations where partners remarry and establish a happy home for their newly created instant family. Such successes, however, do not negate the fact that fathers are spending less time with their children whether they are part of a family that has stayed together or one that has broken up and reformed in another structure.

2. EVENT FATHERS

In recent times a new term has been devised to describe another kind of fathering. 'Event fathers' are those who proudly say they attend all their children's sports carnivals, school presentations and formal occasions. While this is a good thing for both father and child, life is not defined by events. In any case, these occurrences always turn out the same way. Although they're primarily for the children, invariably the parents congregate and use the event as their social function and not a chance to interact with their kids. Even then, the events themselves tend to have a formal structure to them, not allowing fathers in particular to make contact with their children informally about what is going on at school.

While attending events is important, for all the drawbacks, taking part in a normal day when few parents are around provides a better way of understanding what goes on at your child's school. Life at school is not made up of major events but rather a regular day-by-day ritual. Unfortunately, few fathers take time out of their schedules to visit school to take part in programs during the day. Even the '100 per cent attendance' event fathers rarely volunteer for such activities.

3. PHANTOM FATHERS

Another common term of recent times is 'phantom fathers' (not the kind who walk with ghosts). These fathers profess their great love of their children and always have a number of recent family photos on their desks. They seem to be dedicated fathers and yet somehow they are never around. They work long hours, miss all meals at home, travel extensively and work weekends. They keep saying how much they want to be great dads and yet they fail the basic test. They do not make time for their families in their work schedules. They are utterly blind and unresponsive to their families' needs. Yet somehow they are able to continue to be focused on their work and be seen by others as caring fathers.

4. EXECUTIVE FATHERS

Many of these are phantoms without knowing it. Recently at a conference in Sydney on fatherhood, someone I knew delivered a paper on corporate leaders as fathers. The speaker was a classic workaholic. He was still in his late thirties, had three young children and nonetheless worked very long hours during the week and regularly on weekends. Yet here was this man who only recognised his family because of the photos on his desk up on stage talking about how he had been able to be both a corporate leader and a great father. What was most troubling was that there may have been some father in the audience looking for guidance on how to manage the diverse priorities of work and family who may have been taken in by the speech by this phantom father and be set on a totally erroneous course. Phantom fathers, executive or otherwise, are really charlatans, taking on the guise of loving, attentive fathers but not delivering when it counts. They send confusing signals to other fathers. They are of more concern than the man who dismisses his children outright, because at least with this type of father it is clear what his real priorities are. With the phantom father all that we get is humbug.

The Trouble with Larry

'**L**arry seems to really love his kids and he also maintains his commitment to the job. See, you *can* have it all.'

This model of an executive father who is consistently successful at work and also able to maintain a healthy relationship with his family is very rare. A study in the U.S. of 300 founders of major companies noted that these men were able to maintain successful companies and develop remarkably good relationships with their families. But it also found that it was their unique position as owners of their companies that allowed them to decide their work ethic as opposed to be driven by it. The same can't be said for the significant majority of senior executives who work in companies they do not own, reporting to management and boards they do not control.

Generally speaking, fathers who attempt to meet all of their executive work commitments will undermine their family relationships in the process. Larry does not have it all; he just makes everyone think he does.

An interesting trend may also suggest that there exists a level of parental guilt with regard to time spent with children. In 1980 in the U.S. $US6.7b was spent on toys. By 1995 this had risen to over $US17.5b. In a survey of preschoolers in the U.S. it was found that at Christmas time children asked for, on average, 3.4 presents and yet were given 11.7 presents by their parents. I believe that there is a direct correlation between lack of time spent with children and the increase in such 'guilt' presents. All children love toys and the receipt of an unexpected toy will bring the parent an immediate positive response from the child. All is well, broken promises recovered: not so. Firstly the pattern being established is very unhealthy for both parent and child. The parent begins to believe that material goods can be used as a replacement for time spent with the child, while the child is being taught that the parent believes a present makes up for a commitment to spend time together.

The lasting effect of a particular toy is very very small. The lasting effect of time spent developing a relationship with a child is significant and lifelong.

THE EVER-PRESENT BOX

Family time today is often defined by the TV schedule. Television is often an easy answer to the problem of children in the morning—all revved up and nowhere to go. It's easy to switch on cartoons to keep them entertained and quiet. The fact is, however, that watching TV in the morning affects a child's schooling by modifying its initially active brain pattern. Night-times are cloaked in the seriousness of the evening news with sitcoms to follow. There is something quite strange about families sitting around a TV set at night and apparently enjoying each other's company, but without any of the banter and chitchat that used to characterise home life. It is as though families have outsourced their normal intercourse to the television sitcoms. It's such a perfect solution that it even caters for fathers who get home late from work. The rest of the family can still sit around the set and enjoy the family banter of a sitcom even though Dad's not home. A perfect model of the efficient, economically rational household.

The rapid increase in the use of personal computers and the internet and the explosion in available channels through pay TV has provided even more opportunities for our children to opt out of engaging with their family. Communication is lost when families sit down to watch television together. They don't interact and they don't share anything. It also ensures that children stay nice and quiet, if not catatonic. My own experience is that when I come home from work and the kids have not been watching television, they are more alert, more open to talking about their day and generally more active. But when they're watching television they seem to be in a form of trance, slow and lethargic and not really interested in what is going on around them. Maybe that is just my family and maybe we are unique. Maybe not.

CLOCKING KID-TIME

So how much time is actually spent with children these days? Suspicious of previous data based on estimates provided by mothers and fathers, the American researchers Rebelsky and Hanks installed microphones in the homes of parents of newborn children. They found that fathers, on average, interacted directly with their babies for 37.7 seconds a day! These fathers had thought they were spending at least fifteen to twenty minutes a day with them. Burgess reports that these findings have been recently reaffirmed by similar tests.

In a study entitled 'Facilitating Future Changes', J.H. Pleck and M.E. Lamb discuss research into the possible sources of men's low participation in family life compared to that of women. This suggests that men's work is not by itself a sufficient explanation. The amount of time they spend in paid work does have an impact on the amount of time spent with the family. Other social factors such as taking after one's own father, social attitudes, lack of support from wives or peers and inadequate parenting skills also play a part. But even allowing for these influences, the main reason why men spend so little time with their families appears to be that they don't really want to go home.

Other researchers have found that the tension between work and family is heightened when both elements are strong, though one will always ultimately prevail. On the other hand, if an executive feels a much stronger pull towards his work commitments than to his family, then no amount of pressure from his spouse or children will make him change his ways. Only if he is really sensitive to the importance of his family responsibilities will he put them ahead of his work. Often it depends on the relative rewards they offer. Work provides very clear and easily recognised rewards—money, power and possibly fame. The rewards offered by home and family are less easy to measure, except by such intangible factors as the development of a close relationship between a father and his children by establishing an intimacy with them in their early years that continues through the difficulties of adolescence and hopefully survives into their maturity and the rest of their lives. That in itself is its own reward.

MEN AND WOMEN: DIFFERENT WANTS

In a society with so many conflicting and confusing modes of behaviour it is hard to determine what people really want to do with their lives. According to the sociologist H. Glezer, in an article on 'Juggling Work and Family Commitments', when parents were asked whether they would prefer to work full-time, part-time or not at all, eighty per cent of men preferred full-time work, fifteen per cent part-time and five per cent said they would prefer not to work. However, only eighteen per cent of women wanted full-time work, with fifty-eight per cent preferring part-time work and twenty-four per cent saying they would rather not be in employment at all. It would appear that men were doing what they wanted to do—that is, working full-time— while the majority of women would have been happier in part-time work.

In an interesting study, L. Duxbury and C. Higgins investigated differences between the sexes in their attitudes to the question of work and family. They found that women are more likely than men to:

- put family demands before personal needs;
- feel guilty if they perceive that their role as provider takes away from their time as nurturer;

• exhibit greater concern and stress if they feel that they are neglecting their partners.

Men will be more likely than women to see being a good provider as key to their role in the family. They will also be more likely to think that their family interferes with their work.

HOME MUMS AND CAREER MUMS

Australian society is increasingly tending to devalue the work of raising a family. In what are meant to be enlightened times women who choose to spend time at home rather than pursuing a career are often looked at as having given up their real calling. In the process of making sure that women have a choice when they become mothers, we have subtly suggested that women who work outside the home rather than at home raising kids are somehow smarter and more valuable. We should support both choices, but I fail to see how choosing to spend one's time helping develop the next generation is not in fact the most valued job.

I recall having a heated argument a few years ago with a lawyer friend of mine. She had chosen to continue work when she had a baby, while my wife had chosen to stay at home and look after the children. My lawyer friend asked what my wife did. I replied that she was at home with the children, to which the lawyer responded: 'Is that all?' I guess in retrospect she was just in the wrong place at the wrong time.

We then spent quite some time discussing the relative merits of working mums versus 'at home' mums. What was most annoying about the discussion was that she could not accept that deciding to stay at home with your children was a choice that some women make and that this choice should not be seen as having 'taken the easy road'. Her position was that she needed to work and that she couldn't imagine 'wasting her talents' by staying at home with her children. I applaud women who are able to balance a successful work life with the responsibility of raising children—especially in a society that continues to place the major responsibility for child-rearing on the mother. At the same time I do not accept that there is any 'right' choice. While applauding working mums I also applaud mums who decide that the best use of their skills and energy is to stay at home with their children. This is in no way an easy choice. It is one that takes a woman out of an environment (work) where rewards are clear and each day has structure. She is removed from an environment of continual contact with adults and one where she can have some independence. The choice to stay at home is a very hard one. The 'stay at home' mum has determined that while she is making significant trade-offs in her life she is doing the best for her children.

While ensuring women continue to have the choice we must establish a more balanced approach to valuing the choices made.

A MOTHER'S ROLE?

For some time I have watched the way in which stay-at-home mothers were being looked down upon by the 'career' mothers who were able to hold down a major job and be a great mum. Nobody is standing up to defend the mothers who really believed they were doing the best thing for their families by being at home for them. There are no business-suited, well-coiffured corporate women defending their choice with any passion. The issue is not in fact which way of life is better, but executive mothers and their supporters should accept that being a mother at home is perhaps just as important a role as any corporate job.

In *The Time Bind* Hochschild found that implicit in work-family conflict at Amerco was the devaluation of the work of raising a family. As a consequence individuals studied consciously tried to escape the work of child rearing in favour of the paid work environment.

WRAPPING UP

This chapter has been arguing that we are on the wrong track. The facts speak for themselves: the decreasing time spent by fathers with children is having a detrimental effect on children. Further, children are not developing an ability to understand the role of fathers and men in society because fathers are so seldom with them. The values we are promoting in our society are more focused on economic wealth than on any sense of social wellbeing. We are allowing ourselves to be sucked into believing work and money are in fact the most important things in life. They are not.

What is most important in life is the way one looks at and takes care of one's family, in the broadest sense. If we truly believed in the importance of looking after our children and each other and we were prepared to act accordingly, the world would be a better place. If fathers took more responsibility for their children, spent more time with them and opened their hearts to them, and to their spouses as well, we would be well on the way to creating a better and more humane world. It is as simple and complex as that.

If you take only one thing from this chapter, let it be the point that as a father you have a responsibility to your children and yourself to spend more time with them. You and they alike will benefit from this commitment.

2

In search of a balanced life

As we have seen, under-fathering is particularly pronounced among the higher ranks of corporate management. There is no doubt that if executive fathers lived a life where their energy and resources were properly balanced between their work, their family and their personal interests, they would spend a lot more time with their children. This would occur not just because of the extra time they would have as such, but because the more time you spend with children the more you *want* to spend with them. Nor is under-fathering the only outcome of the unbalanced lives of our executive workforce. Spousal relationships and personal friendships suffer equally. The life of the 'busy executive' becomes one ruled by work, lived for work, lived at work.

To argue that a life spent focused on work is probably not the best way to spend one's existence, it must first be proved that a balanced life is a desirable goal. But why should this be so? It all depends on what you see as the meaning of life and how you think it should be lived. If you were to map the day-by-day schedule of our business leaders, you could easily be excused for concluding that they believed work was the sole reason for living. If this is so, then such people should never marry or have children. They clearly have no intention of honouring their obligations and responsibilities either as husbands or fathers.

Human beings are complex creatures and have consequently erected an extremely complex set of social structures around themselves. They function on many different levels—not just as individuals, couples or parents but members of a wider community as well, participating in its manifold activities as closely as possible, not for any monetary reward but for the satisfaction of cooperating with other people towards some common end. To reduce life simply to a process of work and nothing else is thus to devalue and degrade it, especially when it is not a question of sheer economic necessity, as is often the case for the less fortunate who are living a very tenuous existence. It does not apply to the men who manage our companies and corporations. They can't hide behind the excuse of the 'provider'. These people have been driven to believe that they must give more and more to work, until nothing else in life matters to them.

THE SPILLOVER SYNDROME

Research into work-family balance has found three major forms of work-family conflict; a) time-based conflict; b) strain-based conflict; c) behaviour-based conflict. Not surprisingly work-family conflict is found to be related to hours worked. Combined with this definition of the different types of conflict is the concept of 'spillover'. More often than not spillover is found to occur in one direction for working men. Work problems spill over into the home environment. This happens far more often than the reverse scenario of family problems spilling over into the work environment.

When a man comes home and goes into his study to continue work, he is clearly cutting himself off from his family and its issues. But it's even more worrying when he comes home with no apparent work in tow but with his head full of unresolved work problems. He may attempt to join in things and make some effort to communicate with the rest of the family, but his mind will really be elsewhere, resulting in tiffs and blow-ups over minor domestic matters that are actually caused by his office concerns. Children will react warily to such a confusing situation and even perhaps start to avoid their father until they're able to tell whether he had come home free of his work problems or has brought them back with him.

The more strain a father experiences at work the greater this spillover becomes and even the small amount of time he's able to spare with his children will be lost and wasted. Some fathers can use the trip home to 'decompress' from the day's activities, but many senior executives carry their work worries around in their heads not only overnight but during the weekend and even on holidays. In such situations work has never really stopped and the family is given the very clear message that the job comes first.

The worst thing about such utter obsessiveness is that a man might sign up to the doctrine of 'work first' only to find out in his last years of existence that this was a huge mistake. It is too late once your children are grown up, your wife has left you and your friends have deserted you to realise that just maybe life was not really about dedicating the majority of your waking moments to work. This realisation has to occur early enough for any possible damage to relationships to be repaired, if not avoided altogether.

A BURNT-OUT CASE

When I first started work in the computer industry in the early 1980s, I met a man who had been working in a senior sales position with the company for many years. Although he looked as though he was in his fifties he was actually only forty-odd. He seemed tired, old, dispirited. As I found out, his story was one of dedication to his work. He had been moved around the world by the company, spending a few years in each place. At the time I met him he and his family had just returned to Australia. They had long ago lost contact with their friends in Australia and their family was breaking up because the children did not cope well with the constant moving. While still trying to readjust to life back in Australia this man continued to work incredibly long hours at the office. Then one day he was let go. I am not sure of the reasons, but I suspect that it was because the trend was to hiring younger, more energetic sales people and this man was now no longer able to deliver. He had spent a lifetime dedicated to the company, allowing it to dictate not only where his family lived but also how his family developed. In the end I remember him reflecting on how foolish he had been to allow himself to be caught up in doing what the company wanted and not what was best for him and his family. Here was a fundamentally good person who had made the mistake of believing that companies always had their employees' interests at heart. Perhaps he was naïve or just too trusting.

There are, of course, many examples of men who make the same mistake, but on the basis of self-interest rather than being sucked in by company rhetoric. The man mentioned above worked very long hours and then spent what was left of the day at home. But I've known other men who don't even do that.

A Tragedy Waiting to Happen

Some time back I spent some time with one of the fathers at my eldest daughter's school. This man works in the financial services industry, which is notorious for 'dedication to work' encompassing not so much time at the office but 'social interaction' with clients. While socialising with clients may well be part of the mating dance required to secure major pieces of business, this particular man has turned it into an art form. He has two children, one at school and one at home. His wife stays at home to look after them.

His working day is defined by being at the office by 8 a.m. for the market briefing. He is rarely home before 7.30 p.m. and he spends at least two nights a week out late with clients, while one day of the weekend is taken up by golf. He also regularly takes long weekends to go on 'boys' adventures'. He attends perhaps twenty-five per cent of the school events (sports carnivals, concerts, Education Week events). When I have seen him with his children he seems attentive, and yet he equally seems comfortable in not seeing much of them (or his wife). I have tried to talk to him about what he may be missing out on and what he is perhaps depriving his children of, all with little effect. His response is always that he himself never saw his father but he still felt he had a great childhood because of the presence of his older brothers. He simply refused to accept that perhaps he had a distorted view of what made up a family and the responsibilities of fatherhood. Probably the most disturbing thing was the way he would go out on the town at the drop of a hat but could rarely see his way clear to devote a couple of hours a term to attend a school function. He would often argue that these social events were critical to his success. He would not accept that perhaps missing one to be home early to be with his family was a worthwhile and reasonable trade-off. Nor would he accept that he could miss one morning of work every three months so that he could better understand his children.

His life is completely out of balance. Although he allocates his time well between real work and socialising (under the guise of work), he gives very little time and practically no energy to his wife and children. There is a chance that he will never grow up and will go to his grave the little boy he still in fact is. More likely, however, as he approaches retirement he will begin to see the sacrifices he has made for work. But by then it will be too late to try to turn things around. His life will have been spent pursuing the next great boys' night out or the next great footy game, not questioning what else mattered until near the end.

BALANCED KIDS, UNBALANCED ADULTS

Many of my old school and university friends who aspired for senior management positions have led very unbalanced lives. Their urge to get to the top has caused them to give up all other interests and in many cases give up being involved fathers.

When kids are small they are constantly introduced to new activities by their parents. Parents are always trying to ensure their children's lives are balanced between leisure and schooling, between passive and active pastimes, between individual and collective pursuits. If little Johnny has been watching too much television then his mother or father will turn off the TV and suggest he goes outside and plays. Children don't naturally understand that they need to balance their day with other activities. Many would stay glued to the television all their waking hours if they could. As parents we know this is not a good thing to encourage and so we try to ration the amount of time they spend watching television and videos. Similarly, when Mary has been studying long hours for her HSC her parents will break in and suggest she take a break and go and see a movie, play some sport or just relax with friends. These are just a couple of examples of parents helping their children through their formative years.

It seems as parents we want our children to experience a balanced life while they are growing up. We try to instil in them a sense that they should maintain a wide range of interests and not let any of them predominate. Yet something seems to go wrong when people start work—-

especially in professional or managerial careers. A lifetime of education about the need for balance is thrown out the door in favour of commitment to the job. No amount of time is enough, until the client is happy. A number of friends of mine at senior levels in legal and investment banking firms, for instance, are never away from work. They are always on call for their clients. None of their superiors ever tell them to lighten their workload and try to spend more time with their wives and children. Forget balance, the message is—what we want is commitment. It is so contrary to every normal human standard. We spend years helping our children learn about the many facets of life only to have them jettison the doctrine once they enter the workplace and replace it with one based on the worship of money.

THE THREE AGES OF (CORPORATE) MAN

In an article in the journal *Organisational Dynamics* in 1979, the American researchers Evans and Bartolome discussed a survey of 532 middle managers who had attended various executive development programs at INSEAD, a leading business school in Switzerland. They concluded that managers dealt with the ambivalence inherent in their lifestyles by limiting their focus of attention and concern to one or a few parts of their lives at any one stage. In the first stage, from their mid-twenties to mid-thirties, their main concern was launching a career. During this stage they were found to become quite obsessive about work performance and upward mobility. Trading off personal interests or family commitments was seen as a justifiable sacrifice for career success. In most cases those men still in their mid-twenties had not yet taken on significant family commitments and if they were married it tended to be to someone who was also in the workforce. Such a home environment was conducive to concentrating their energies on their careers.

The second stage, from the mid-thirties to early forties, was marked by the development of a greater interest in personal matters. But this was less pronounced in men on the way to senior or executive positions, who tended to maintain their obsessive work commitment. Stage three, from the mid-forties into the fifties, was characterised either by an integration of professional and private life (generativity) or by resignation to a more fragmented style of life (maintenance). Examples of men who have resigned themselves to a fragmented life abound in Australian senior business management. It is hard to find many cases of a healthy integration of private and professional life.

A BIG MAC LOOKS BACK

Peter Ritchie, chairman of McDonald's Australia, recently made some interesting comments about his time in management. He now realised, he said, that his near-complete devotion to his work was detrimental to both himself and his family and he looked back with some regret at how he conducted himself as a family man in the course of his career. He is now looking at ways in which McDonald's can ensure current managers are more balanced in their approach to work and family.

While there have been some examples like Peter Ritchie they are few and far between. My most common experience of men in this third stage is that they strongly support the idea of the remote father 'because of the demands of the job'. In some instances they make a feeble attempt to justify a life which they know in fact is completely out of joint. But others actually seem to believe it is good for men not to be around their children and that a father should normally be out working, even if this means working all the time.

The three stages of life described by Bartolome and Evans also applies to the Australian corporate world. During the early years of their careers, it is probably quite reasonable for new employees to throw themselves into their jobs. Trading personal time for work allows them to create a solid base for their careers and release some of their youthful energy. What is wrong is for managers to allow their staff to continue this ethic and in fact promote such an approach to work as being desirable. We should let our younger employees have some time to become immersed in their careers, but then we should require them to start to balance their lives. In the latter part of stage one balance may only mean looking after one's personal interests, as well as work, or it may flow also to maintaining a healthy relationship. By the time stage two arrives and some of these people are moving into senior roles, a criterion for promotion should be a sense of balance and how to manage all aspects of their lives, not just their performance in the work environment.

PART-TIME WORK, FULL-TIME LIFE

Some years ago, when I first started to question the work ethic in the business environment and attempted to discuss the need for a more balanced approach my actions were interpreted as meaning that I wanted to give up and no longer had the drive or energy to focus on the company. Even more recently, when I changed from full-time to part-time work, I noticed that people automatically assumed I had given up and lost my drive.

This type of response is really a statement of values. Now that I am no longer working full time, I do not have any more time on my hands than I did when I was working sixty hours a week. Through contracting my work (private equity and strategic consulting) to three days a week I am fortunate to be able to devote the balance of the working week to charitable causes and other community activities. In reality, I apply the same energy, focus and intellect to the charitable causes and see this as 'work', so my working week is still in the order of forty-five hours per week, but I have the flexibility to manage the week to incorporate time with my family. In fact, I often find that I am more tired from trying to juggle many activities than when I was prepared to sacrifice all for the job.

I no longer attempt to explain this to friends who continue a sixty-hour work schedule, as they believe that time spent doing anything but 'real work' can't be tiring or stressful and that 'other' activities couldn't possibly present the same level of strain. But obviously it depends on individual attitudes. If you are the type of father who thinks 'taking care of the kids' means lying on the lounge watching hours of football on TV while your kids disappear somewhere, then I agree you will have a pretty stress-free existence. If on the other hand you treat the opportunity to be with your children as a time when you can interact with them, learn from them and teach them, then you are naturally going to exert yourself. This stuff can be tiring. Just ask any mother who is at home with her children at the end of the school holidays!

ENJOYMENT AND ENERGY

I am not suggesting that fathers (and mothers) should not have time to do whatever they want. Personal time is as important as family time in an individual's life. It's just that one is not necessarily the other. Dragging your kids to some event that you love and they hate is not family time— it's your time. Just make sure you can be honest about what type of activity you are undertaking and whom it is really for.

The same can be said of how you approach community activities or other interests. There is no reason why you can't throw as much energy and commitment into these activities as you do into your work. In fact, to do anything less suggests that work is in fact the most important thing in your life—because that is where you put more of your energy and commitment. The great fallacy of the work ethic is that doing anything other than being at work is easy. Other activities may be more enjoyable or be more fulfilling, but they do not take less commitment or less energy.

Executives and managers readily admit that success in business demands sacrifice and that the most common sacrificial lamb is family involvement. Some executives, however, can succeed in business and yet still maintain balanced, healthy and deep relationships with their family and children.

WHAT'S IT ALL ABOUT?

A realisation of the need for balance can come through thinking about what life is all about. This is sometimes difficult as people find it hard to quantify all the parts of their lives and thus are unable to change their normal patterns of behaviour. But another way to focus on goals other than those generated by work is to try to think about how you want to be remembered once you are gone. This may uncover the uncomfortable fact that the course our life is taking is not in fact leading where we want it to end. Life presents so many daily dramas and distractions that the end goal can easily be lost.

This focus on the end of your life may seem a little depressing, but it's reasonable enough to assume that our lives do have some purpose. While taking up space on this planet it seems a desirable goal both to enjoy oneself and leave something of value behind. The legacy may well be nothing more than having been a person who was considerate of others. Some people will aspire to solving some of the world's great problems as a product of their lives. Finding a cure for cancer, addressing the problem of poverty in Africa or Asia, helping to achieve human rights in places like China or acting to protect the world's environment from future destruction are goals that transcend a single person's life. Without the effort of individuals progress would not be made in areas critical to the future of the world. It is difficult to criticise the obsessive work ethic of people whose efforts will be measured on such a scale, nor is it fair to suggest their lives should be more balanced. At some point perhaps the goodness they do may even be more important than a solid father-child relationship.

The reality, of course, is that very few people are actually involved in projects of such global significance. Most of us work for varying degrees of remuneration in jobs that can at times be exciting, at other times dull. Yet many people approach their work as if it was in fact decisive for the ongoing survival of the human race.

MAKING IT MATTER

I am not suggesting that workers in any field should not feel positive about what they are doing. But it all needs to be kept in perspective. Most jobs matter in the sense that they perform some socially useful function, from the practical help provided to other people as part of their daily duties by nurses, firemen, police and ambulance officers and so forth to the less easily identifiable contribution of economists in the backrooms of government departments and company offices. Yet in all these cases and the dozens in between there is clearly no suggestion that if individuals worked ten per cent fewer hours the wheels of society would fall off. This seems obvious, but what we see is increasing commitments to work often tied not to greater social benefit but to the objective of making more money.

We have also created a work environment where people are expected to 'believe in the dream', 'smash the competitor', 'beat those targets'. It propagates a sense that every minute spent on every task is critical to the progress of the world.

The work environment does not reward balance. Rewards are tied to the work performance and increasingly work performance is measured in terms of some financial goals (sales, profitability, share growth). The rewards system motivates people to work to whatever lengths possible to achieve financial goals, as does the promotions system. It would be naï veto expect that companies will suddenly start to measure how 'balanced' their employees are and reward them accordingly. Apart from the difficulties of quantifying the concept, this could never happen because it runs counter to the expectations of shareholders (more profits, more dividends). Thus any change in behaviour will be the result of individual managers who attempt to marry some degree of business success with a more balanced approach to work or, more significantly, decisions by individuals to trade financial rewards for a more balanced life.

Microsoft Part 1

Microsoft is a company renowned for both its products and its financial performance. In terms of setting corporate strategy, understanding new markets, developing successful business and managing growth, Microsoft is worthy of praise. Many companies could learn a lot from how Microsoft manages its business. Yet in some ways it suffers the same problems as many other companies across a variety of industries. When I first started as managing director of Microsoft Australia, my obsession with work and the whole work ethic was at its peak. Yet even at this time, while I believed (and still do) that working at Microsoft meant that you were part of something that was changing the face of business, I did not expect people to trade in their lives for the company. The environment we tried to create was one where people believed in the work we were doing but at the end of the day everyone understood it was still just a job. Our performance was as good as, if not better than, all other subsidiaries around the world and we were able to maintain a focus on balance.

In retrospect, I realise that while management talked a lot about balance we did not do very much to help the employees better manage their lives. We did encourage telecommuting and a regime of no weekend work, but we did not explore fully how to ensure that employees were able to function properly as spouses and parents as well as employees. I know some will argue that it is not the employer's business to worry about what happens to employees outside the work environment. Such a position is too simplistic. Work is invading people's lives to an ever-greater extent and employers therefore have a responsibility to think about their employees as human beings, not just as corporate resources. Of course, the test of any company in this regard would be the extent to which it would increase costs to provide assistance to employees outside work. In our case we were moving in the right direction philosophically, but our progress was slow.

One difference I noticed between our operation and that of company headquarters in Redmond, U.S., was the sense that it was just a job. A good job. A well-paid job. A job providing exciting and interesting challenges—but still just a job. When I said this in Australia people seemed to understand what I meant. I was not advocating a lack of commitment as a key qualification in new recruits. I wanted people to be very committed but to first have their life priorities worked out. Basically I felt I could not trust individuals to be managers if they did not have some sense of a balanced life. People who were 100 per cent committed to the company made very bad managers because their view of how to manage people was completely conditioned by what was good for the company and often the needs of an employee are not perfectly aligned with those of the company. A manager who is able not only to get the most from his or her people but to help them develop by allowing for human frailty is of much more value.

When I first made these comments at Redmond I was greeted with much scepticism. Microsoft was defined by its obsessive work culture and under all the fuzzy human relations handouts lived a company whose success was geared to the fact that people put it and its business goals ahead of their families. Nobody ever mandated this in a corporate memorandum, but the culture of the place said, 'We are open twenty-four hours'. The running joke at the time was that if you worked at Microsoft you only worked half-time. You just had to decide which twelve hours of the day that you wanted to work. People could not resolve the conflict between being committed to a job and keeping one's life priorities unaffected by this commitment. To most, commitment to the company was not unlike being in a war situation where the company's survival was tightly linked to personal survival. There was a sense that if we did not ship a product on a particular day then the world would crash in. There was a contradiction between the true social benefit of the work being done and what was being expected in terms of commitment. By shipping the next version of Word or Excel we were not going to cure AIDS or cancer, and while this did not mean we should not care I found this obsession with such artificial goals disconcerting.

Perhaps there were a few people at Microsoft who were doing work of a world-changing nature. Bill Gates, Nathan Mhyrvold (chief scientist) and Paul Maritz (head of the Operating Systems group) were changing the face of computing and possibly the face of business. Maybe there were ten or twenty more. The rest of the 10,000 staff at the time were executing difficult, stressful jobs that were just that—jobs. While people at Redmond found my position strange, equally I felt as though they needed to grow up. Youthful obsession is fine for a while, but eventually you have to take responsibility for your life and the lives of those close to you.

I have since found a similar approach to work and exaggerated sense of urgency in Australian business that is quite divorced from the real importance of the tasks being undertaken or the timeframe required for their completion.

PLAYING FOR THE ENDGAME

So what is the endgame, the final goal, the place that everyone wants to be when he or she takes the last great leap? Ask this question of a few friends over a bottle of wine and the responses are deep and meaningful. To provide a great environment for one's children or leave a legacy behind that has helped the community in some way are two of the most common. Others which are perhaps less philosophical and yet more honest include wanting to leave behind a successful company which continues to thrive thereafter—and in one sad case that of a colleague who wanted to have more money than his friends when he died. Work that one out!

Unfortunately, more often than not people seem stumped by such a question. Too much of their energy and time is taken up by meeting the requirements of their employer, coupled with those of their family, to allow them to think of the future. Life is lived day to day with no clear plan in sight. Such a pragmatic approach has its risks— most significantly that you end up living a life that on reflection you did not want to live. It's a bit late to ask for a different piece of music to dance to once the dance is over.

It's much more difficult to attempt to answer this question and then structure your life around your answer than just live and let life lead you. When you let your life be defined by your work experience you are released from the responsibility of determining a path forward and what your life should mean. It's an easy approach that works well for the employer and sometimes for the employee. The employee succumbs to the push and pull of the job and either drags his family in behind the work demands or cuts them free to exist in a place that is unaffected by 'Dad's work'. Either model is wrong because both have allowed the individual to forgo his responsibilities.

WORK OUT A LIFE PLAN

In attempting to determine where you want your life to lead, you are forced to make plans which are quite distinct from those for your career. Of course a job will affect one's life plan. The key thing is that a life plan is not defined by one's role or job but by the overall goal of the individual. While this may be difficult to work out, it can be just as disconcerting for the employer, who suddenly finds he no longer has the same semi-mystical hold he once exercised over the employee. The employee can now see through the extravagant demands of the employer and hence take greater control of his own life. By the same token, he can no longer use the company as an excuse for not fulfilling his family and other personal responsibilities.

If you can succeed in achieving a satisfactory balance between your career, your family and your own personal goals, you will be well on the way to leading a fully rounded life. It is likely that your company employers will not be of great assistance to you. They will continue to propagate the myth of the work ethic, beating up the latest task as something of the importance of curing a major disease. Companies will always be focused on the returns they can achieve through the efficient use of their assets in the form of increased profitability rather than helping their employees to spend less time at work and gain a new perspective on how important work really is. Achieving a balanced life will be the product of individual effort. You may have some friends or colleagues who share your desires and goals, but this is basically a personal adventure.

BREAKING THE EXECUTIVE BIND

The first sign of progress will be if you realise your life is out of kilter and you want to get more balance. Yet my experience suggests that most men whose lives are out of balance do not recognise it. Firstly, let's look at the scope of responsibilities for most senior executives.

Once you are married with children your life has some fairly clear parts to it:

- Job/career
- Relationship with spouse or partner
- Relationship with children

- Relationship with other family members and friends
- Pursuit of personal interests and hobbies

In no necessary order of importance you first have your career—the means by which you can express your creativity, enhance some God-given skill, or just earn the money you need in order to live. Within executive groups I know the career or job is described more as a life in itself than just a job. The subtitle to Arlie Hochschild's book *The Time Bind—When Work Becomes Home and Home Becomes Work* defines this situation accurately.

Then you have a set of relationships with family members and friends. These relationships are partly a responsibility, but the obligations involved are reciprocal. Without constant maintenance they die off.

Finally, there is the pursuit of personal interests. Making more of a success of your job does not count as a personal interest. This is the realm of sports, hobbies and other interests which allow you to learn new skills and do things you really enjoy.

Quickie Quiz

If you haven't yet realised that your life is out of balance then take the following quick quiz:

- Are you unhappy with the nature of your relationship with your children or spouse?
- Are you involved with work related activities for more than 50 hours a week?
- Has it been more than a week since you spent more

than two hours talking with one of your children?
- Of the last five social events you attended were more than three work-related?
- Did you take less than four weeks' annual leave last year?
- Do you spend less than three hours a week on some personal hobby?
- Are you regularly not home for dinner with the children?

If you answered more than one of the questions above with a YES then your life is out of balance.

WRAPPING UP

In Chapter 9 a process for documenting a life plan is presented and discussed. The goal of the plan is to ensure the establishment of a balanced life. The reality is you can only start to develop a more balanced life if you allocate the time to develop the other aspects of your life. Desire is one thing: action is far more impressive.

Achieving a level of balance in your life between your career, your family and your personal interests will make you a better father, employer and spouse. It will also make you a happier person and someone who has found new meaning in his life. More on this later . . .

3
My wake-up call

Everyone knows what a wake-up call is. We have all used the facility in hotels to make sure we make the early flight or meeting, or even sometimes at home to back up the alarm clock. It snaps us out of sleep and gets us on our feet to try to face the new day.

There is another use of the term which is more relevant here. Many people who have gone through a near-death experience talk about the 'wake-up call' effect it has had upon them and how their lives are now different as a result.

Interestingly, people who have been close to death rarely come back to say they are really keen to work longer hours and make more money.

In all cases they describe their change of attitude as one involving the need to get closer to their families, be a better and more involved spouse or parent, spend more time on community activities, get a job they really enjoy, be nicer to people around them and try to make up for things they feel guilty about in the past.

THE TRAP OF THE TREADMILL

What does this pattern tell us? Surely it says that if taken off our daily treadmill we would all admit we are doing a less than fantastic job as a father, friend, husband and citizen. Vowing to turn our performance around in these areas also suggests that we are somewhat ashamed of our track record up until the warning call came.

A major part of our daily treadmill is the work environment and in the case of white-collar executives the job often defines their total existence outside sleeping and eating.

CAREER REWARDS VERSUS HOME REWARDS

The momentum created at work carries over to the individual's time at home, accentuated both by peer pressure and the enticements of the work reward system. It's widely recognised that people weigh the rewards and benefits of one form of activity against those of another before deciding which to concentrate on. When net family rewards are lower in value than net career rewards the individual will invest more heavily in career than family.

All men would claim that their families are the most important thing in their lives, but I know many who are nonetheless very quick to accept late night and weekend meetings, frequent travel and important company social events such as golf without even questioning the sacrifices entailed as regards family time. I have often argued that a company social golf day really should not be seen as more important than being home to tuck your children into bed, let alone attending a variety of school functions.

DANGLING THE CORPORATE CARROT

However, the work environment delivers clear and immediate rewards in the form of accolades for a job well done through to bonuses, promotions and enhanced career prospects. On a weekly basis it is evident how you are doing, particularly at senior levels where performance is geared to defined metrics of profit, marketshare, shareholder value and budgeted expense levels.

Not only are these rewards well defined but they are reinforced consistently within the company as well as outside, through reports in the financial press and other media extolling the virtues of our corporate leaders, which only encourage the average executive to expect not only financial success but public acclaim as his due.

HOME, HEARTH AND HAPPINESS

Compare this with the home environment, which offers a degree of stimulation and satisfaction in terms of human and personal relationships which the standard job situation can rarely if ever hope to emulate. These 'rewards', however, take many years to emerge and develop. If your children want to spend time with you when they grow up, this is in itself reward for the love and attention you showed them when they were young.

The executive whose mind is locked into the short-term focus and immediate reward system of his job faces a major challenge in trying to adjust to the different values of the family. This becomes particularly acute when he has to choose between spending time at work or at home. Obviously most executive work is necessary, but a lot of it is discretionary and not critical to meeting business goals.

Unfortunately, this work obsession can be reinforced by failing to tackle the problem fairly and squarely. If an executive decides to spare his family an extra hour or two of his precious time without throwing his heart into it, the chances are he won't succeed and will conclude the effort doesn't pay off. This will only prove to him that he should maintain his focus on work and its more easily measured reward system.

MAKING TIME FOR SCHOOL

In my experience an executive who receives an invitation to a client's social function is more likely to accept it than take part in a minor school activity, such as taking an infants' reading class or helping out at the canteen. This may be all very well if the latter cuts into the normal working day, but there is no excuse for a father missing a formal school function in which his children are participating. I would rate these events as having the same importance as a high-level executive meeting.

The most interesting thing is the sense of priorities involved. Many of my executive colleagues easily manage their schedules so that they can attend a client's social function, yet somehow they find it beyond them to allocate a couple of hours two or three times a year to attend their children's school to help out in classroom-related activities, let alone formal functions.

In the years my children have been at school on too many occasions I have seen the faces of children who have participated in school functions only to have their father not attend. While these children are always very understanding that their father was too busy at work to attend, their expressions can't hide the sadness they feel.

THE POWER OF PEER PRESSURE ...

Peer pressure is an important factor in the development of such attitudes. Executives often see themselves as members of a social group which exhibits certain values and characteristics. Taking a few hours off to attend a golf day sponsored by an industry supplier is seen as a valuable networking opportunity. Taking time off to drop into your child's school to do some reading or other activity is not seen as beneficial and is thus frowned upon under the value system of the group.

Every young aspiring executive is introduced to the rituals of the 'executive' club whether it's in the form of the much-vaunted golf day or the long lunch, dinner and weekend meetings, extensive overseas travel and general networking across industry. His response to these rituals can establish the degree to which he will be seen as 'someone going somewhere' or merely a plodder who doesn't yet know what it takes to get to the top.

... AND THE NOT-SO-SWEET SMELL OF SUCCESS

Slowly but surely, and against our better judgment, we start to believe that to be a success in the 'hard' world of business you have to be a work-obsessed (defined as working more than sixty hours a week), totally available (i.e. contactable at any time) and aggressive (I'll deal with this later in the book) individual. Success also requires a near-religious devotion to the creation of wealth, as though wealth is the key to wisdom and social savvy.

The result is that most men in the management class are forced to adopt a certain style because they believe that this is what will make other people view them as a success, even though it is in fact a style they don't necessarily agree with.

But to rebel against it would be seen as not wanting to be a success or, even worse perhaps, not wanting to be part of the group. For all the talk of people yearning to be different, the truth is that most of us still choose to be seen as part of a greater mass. In other words, a sense of belonging is a key factor in our lives. Furthermore, many of us fear that failing to conform will make us unemployable and following our inner beliefs will thus result in our not being able to maintain our role as provider for the family.

THE DEEP SLEEP DISORDER

If we think we're going to have a deep night's sleep and have an early morning appointment to keep, we set the alarm to make sure we wake up in time. In the same way, the work environment dulls our senses and prevents us from focusing on the really important aspects of life. It is as though we are in a deep sleep unable to hear the cries for help of our families and friends and even our inner self—until something suddenly snaps us out of our slumber.

Over time we actually begin to believe that a routine of leaving before the kids are up and returning home eleven or twelve hours later, mentally and emotionally exhausted, is a normal sort of life. The kids are in bed or close to it and in any case probably well over the immediate desire to communicate what they felt when they first got home from school. Like any good racehorse you are fed and watered and then you sleep so that you are ready to hit the track again the next morning. The entire organisation of the home front is devoted to supporting your work activity. You are now living to work. You have lost all sight of the fundamental rationale of work—that you work to live.

The deep sleep of your work-driven regimen continues unabated. Occasionally you feel minor guilt at not being home enough but you ease your conscience with the thought that you are providing a great house, nice car, beaut holidays—all better than you had as a kid—and everything in life has a cost. Your family will have to understand that you need to work hard to provide for them. Of course, it is quite likely that you never asked them or perhaps they have also succumbed to a version of your own deep sleep by which they have also now become convinced that your life-in-work is right and proper.

Long ago they gave up wishing that you could attend more school functions and long ago they gave up wondering why you always had your mobile phone with you on family outings. Long ago your wife gave up wishing for more time with you and now looks forward to the trinkets that come as a function of your work effort. Materialism rules.

Then suddenly something terrible happens ...

THE ALARM GOES OFF

You are told by your doctor that you have only a short time to live. A friend or relative dies at a young age. Your wife is stricken by cancer and no-one knows how long she has left.

In particular it is the death of someone close to them that seems to make people see sense. It wakes them up and brings them out of their deep sleep of work obsession. The alarm bells ring loud and clear and suddenly you are able to see life with utter clarity in a way that was not possible only days before. You understand for the first time the problems you have been having with family or friends and you can really measure the importance of your relationship with people around you.

It is during these flashes of enlightenment that people generally decide to change the path their lives are taking. I have rarely met anyone who has been through such an experience and told himself that he should be working eighty hours a week instead of only sixty so that he can make more money for his company. Nor do I know anyone, for instance, who has lost a child in a tragic accident and realises that he had lost touch with her years ago, but then says to himself: 'I must now spend more time away from my other kids so they become even more distant from me.'

Of course, such a response would border on stupidity. Yet it is likely that the executive who was just awakened by a tragic set of circumstances would have continued in his zombie-like work obsession were it not for the call.

Answering the Call

So what happens when a man hears the wake-up call? Invariably he begins to reflect on his life and where he is heading. He looks at his relationship with his children and tries to work out why he no longer knows his kids. Surely it was only yesterday that he was holding his new daughter in his arms? He remembers how he would stare into his beautiful baby's eyes and promise to love and protect her, to give her the time and attention she wanted and needed. He would not be like his father and become a distant parent. He promised to be understanding yet strong, to be involved but not domineering, and most of all to be there when the child needed him.

Suddenly he snaps to present time. He looks at his children. He does not know their teacher, he can't name ten of their friends, and he can't state with any certainty what their opinions are on a range of issues from violence on TV to drugs to teenage sex. More importantly, his children have long ago given up seeking their father out to have a chat, play a game or just have a hug.

How could this have happened? What was the point at which it all changed? The aspirations of the new father turn into the reality of perpetuating the 'remote father' of the previous generation. Here is a man who brings home the bacon, but has no other dimension to his relationship with his children.

He now thinks about his wife. How much in love they were all those years ago. They shared so many common interests and plans for the future. They were vibrant, exciting individuals and yet now the void between them seems immeasurable. He knows that she gave up work to look after the kids but knows little else about the choices his wife has had to make or the pattern of her life now. He has no concept of the turmoil of bath and feed time at night, the claustrophobic environment with little children seemingly permanently attached to her.

He can't understand that the time it takes to be a good mother has meant that his wife had to give up a lot of personal interests. As a couple they no longer share much in common. He can't list the names of her ten best friends, nor can he say what her daily routine is like. As with his children he has become the financial provider who is distant in every other respect.

The survey of his life takes him back to friendships lost over the years. He can't remember when he last spoke to the mates who came to his wedding reception. What happened to break the seemingly cast-iron friendships forged at school and university?

Family, friends, neighbours. Wherever the newly awakened person looks his 'life in review' exhibits the same features. Well-meaning, fervently held visions of the future that were slowly eroded away by his unconscious dedication to the job. The job sapped not only his youth but his passion, energy and ability to give.

This review can and should be quite unnerving. It should shock someone into remembering what life is all about and how badly he has treated so many of the people he purports to love and cherish.

So what happens now?

BLAZING A NEW TRAIL

Many people end up not changing their ways, due to the strength of external pressures which soon pull them back into line. Some, however, do change as a result of their wake-up calls, from a desire to have something more to show for their lives than a good work performance assessment and a new car every few years.

These awakened sleepers set out to blaze a new trail. They start to plan a life for themselves whose main guiding force is a commitment not to the job so much as to the family and to being a full and complete human being. Though work is obviously essential because it provides the financial means for the family to survive, it should nonetheless never be allowed to dominate one's life. This means such things as getting home in time to have dinner with the family and tuck the children into bed, cutting down on evening and other out-of-hours meetings and as much as possible not taking work home at the end of the day or weekends.

A STAR TO STEER BY

Are these people less dedicated? Have they suddenly lost their edge and urge to compete in the 'hard' world of business? Not at all. They remain dedicated to delivering high performances in their careers. The difference is that rather than continuing to be at the beck and call of their jobs they have diligently reviewed how much effort is really required to deliver excellent results and decided to act accordingly. They are efficient performers and should be applauded for their positive and conscientious attitude to their work.

Yet the same manager who would view this person's change in work habits as a lack of commitment would object to paying for ten hours work to fix their car if the job could be done efficiently in five hours.

Instead, however, they are often seen as having 'lost it'— lost their career drive, lost their purpose, lost their hunger or passion. The fact that they may now have a much better relationship with their children and spouses, that they are more active parents in regard to school, that they are looking after their health more, that they have developed interests outside of work and have consequently become more complete human beings seems to have been swamped by the chorus of 'they've lost it'. All the manager has is their pathetic obsession with work. We should rejoice at the breakdown of this obsession and applaud the greater focus on family life and the community it brings.

We should hail such people as examples of how it's possible to change and become better and more complete human beings. We should hold them up as role models for future generations so as to attempt to construct a society that sees life in wider dimensions than just profit and 'hours worked'. They are indeed a star to steer by.

The Miracle of Birth

While the most dramatic form of wake-up call is a death of a relative or friend or a near-death experience, there is one other very common experience which should have the same effect on people.

The birth of a baby is one of the miracles of life. Any father who has been present at the birth of his child can't help but be overcome by the pure magic of the moment. It's almost impossible to describe the emotion you feel as you marvel at the beauty of the birth process and your heightened love and respect for your wife for having gone through the ordeal and delivered this wonderful baby. You have a dramatic sense of responsibility as you realise for the next eighteen or twenty years this little baby will look to you for love, care, protection, direction, moral guidance and wisdom.

Sitting with your wife and baby in the delivery room in the moments after the birth is one of those wake-up calls. In that brief moment your life has changed forever. You are no longer just a friend and husband. You now add the role of father to your responsibilities and this new role you have taken on requires you to review your life and its direction.

Men who miss out on being at the birth of their

children miss one of the most beautiful events that will ever happen in their lives. They will lack something in their understanding of what life is about and the importance of the new role they are taking on.

Holding his newborn baby for the first time gives every father I have met a strong sense of the need to make sure the world is a better place and that his child will have the best he can provide. The same thought processes should lead him to review the more simple aspects of his life, such as how much time and attention he is going to give his wife and family from now on and where he will fit this new child in his list of priorities.

The birth of any child should be the most powerful of wake-up calls for every father and mother. How the father responds to this opportunity to re-examine his life will depend very much on how much he lets his emotions and natural instincts have their play. If he lets them help formulate fundamental changes in the way he views the world then the question of striking a proper balance in his life will become a key goal which he works towards.

If he revels in the beauty of the moment but rationalises away his urge to become a really involved father, then the moment is lost. He will have allowed the twisted logic of 'work over everything' to prevail. The wake-up call has come but the father has hit the snooze button and fallen back into the interminable slumber of a work-directed life.

GETTING IT ALL TOGETHER: A PERSONAL TESTIMONY

My early career was a classic story of youthful energy and ambition. My last university exam was on a Friday and I started my new full time career on the Monday morning. During the first two years I would get to the office by 6.30 a.m. and leave around 7 p.m. I was totally absorbed by the job, the work environment and the company. I would arrive home worn out and unable to muster enough energy to do more than make a quick dinner, do some reading and go to bed. Given I had no family commitments this type of life was fine.

Then I got married and in 1989 our first child was born. I had been Australian managing director of Microsoft for just over a year and I had just turned thirty. In a career sense I was doing very well for my age and the opportunities for me were endless. The temptation to spend more time at work to further this extremely successful career was very strong and yet I felt a very deep sense of responsibility as a father. I knew instinctively that to be a good father I had to spend time with my children—a lot of time.

I started to go to work a little later (around 8:30 a.m.) after spending the early morning with my wife and child. I tried to get home in time to put my daughter to sleep. At first my wife would keep her up until I got home, but of course this proved too stressful on the baby and I missed out on that important special time with her. So I very quickly made a point of being home at least four nights out of five before 6.30 p.m. so that I could put her to bed. The early morning and evening ritual assumed the same importance in my life as any work meeting or function I had to attend.

Increasingly after the birth of my first child I started to think about life very differently, and especially about fatherhood. My first conclusion was that allocating real time—large chunks of it—every day was the basis of being a good father. I realised that the concept of 'quality time' was an excuse used by work-obsessed parents in an effort to delude themselves that they were actually being good parents when in fact they were not.

Small children don't think in terms of quality time. They don't say to themselves, 'Gee, I am really excited about what happened today at pre-school and I can't wait until Dad comes home and I get my twenty minutes of quality time with him. I am going to store up all my enthusiasm, energy and problems until he gets home. In the meantime I'll just wait.' Kids are spontaneous creatures. They also don't think of life as something you need to compress.

Children can take as long as twenty minutes just to tell you about a butterfly they saw that day and how it flew near the dog and how the dog jumped around ...

ALMOST HALFWAY THERE ...

Looking back now, I think I was partially enlightened about what life was about, but I still let my career rule too much of my life. When I made appointments to see people (i.e. people who wanted to see me), I accepted meeting times which, if they ran over, would encroach on my family time. I took too much work home on the weekend (any weekend work is too much!) and I still travelled too much (anything more than three or four weeks a year is way too much).

My first wake-up call had had some effect on my strategy and priorities for life, but looking back now I see I did not change enough.

However, I did learn one other great lesson, which was how to maximise the time I was at work. I learnt to make meetings less frequent and more efficient and I made sure my working day was generally as productive as possible. I still believe the way in which I organise my time allows me to accomplish more than many people who work many more hours than I do.

My career continued to progress and I moved to Seattle, U.S., as a general manager and then vice-president of Microsoft. Corporate headquarters had a similar 'hours worked' ethic to that of many obsessive Australian businesses and I was constantly torn between 'doing the right thing' at work and attending late night meetings and weekend work retreats and my deep-seated belief that I should be spending more time with my child and my wife.

... AND THEN THE FINAL CALL

My next wake-up call was a very cruel one.

In December 1992 my only sister was killed in a car accident in Australia. Travelling in the car with her were her six-month-old daughter and her husband. Her daughter suffered a number of serious injuries, many of which required extensive surgery. Her husband was also injured in the accident.

The late-night phone call from my mother to tell me what had happened was the single most significant event in my life. Anyone who has lost someone close to them would understand the shock, anger and deep depression that sets in as a result.

I do not want to discuss here my feelings and emotions at the time of my sister's death, but suffice it to say she was one of the most caring and wonderful people one could ever meet and for the world to lose her was an immense tragedy. For me personally her death marked a critical turning point.

Within a couple of hours of hearing the news I had decided that I needed to get my life in order. I realised I had to sit down and work out my priorities and make sure I addressed them. This was partly from a desire to help my parents and my sister's husband and child in a time of great distress, but it was also an expression of my wanting to become a better father and husband and a more socially involved person. In short, I wanted to make sure that I invested my time and energy in my work, family, friends and the community in general, in the best possible way.

As a result of this sudden self-revelation my wife and I decided to return to Australia. No-one in the corporate world could understand why anyone could give up a vice-presidency at Microsoft's head office to return to a lower-level job in Australia. Unfortunately I started to receive the sort of treatment many people do when they decide to change their life so that they can devote more attention to their family.

After deciding to return to Australia we had another daughter and I remember feeling the same sense of responsibility at her birth as I had at that of my first child. The difference was that I felt a sense of calmness in terms of the pledges I was making to her. I knew I'd made enough changes to my life to guarantee that I'd be able to spend a lot of time with her and especially to be around whenever she needed me.

I returned to run Microsoft's Asia Pacific group and later its Advanced Technology group based in Sydney. By then I had my goals of a balanced life clearly worked out.

While still in full-time employment I worked around forty hours a week and yet I spent a lot of time with my children and my wife and on community matters. The birth of my daughters and the death of my sister served as very powerful wake-up calls. I feel I have responded to them well and although I was very apprehensive when I embarked on this new approach I am now convinced this is how everybody should run his or her life. Since the late 1990s when I modified my work life to incorporate a portfolio of activities, the total amount of time I spend working has decreased to around forty-five hours per week. While I accept I have been very fortunate to be able to do this, I want to stress that my comments and advice in this book relate to fathers working full-time. It is fair to say that from my return to Australia (when I was still working full-time) I have begun to have a more diverse life that is expressed not only in the output of my paid and unpaid work but also in the smile on the faces of my children as they confidently embark on their own life adventures and also in the stronger relationship I have with my wife.

FOR THOSE WHO HAVEN'T HEARD IT YET

Too many of my friends and colleagues who have had children remain as dogmatically committed to their careers as I used to be. It is as if they have not really taken stock of what has happened to their lives and what these new responsibilities entail.

The solution seems so natural to me now in terms of re-evaluating work and family priorities, and yet so many people simply surrender to the demands of work. Perhaps they haven't heard the wake-up call and perhaps it will take a more significant event in their lives to really make them take notice of it.

For those who haven't responded to it yet—even though they may have faintly been aware of it—I think there are some concrete actions you can take to start to build a better life:

1. Try to work in a company where the CEO and your direct manager truly value the importance of the family and of their employees spending time with their families. Further, navigate towards managers who fairly value how long a job should take and how much time is reasonable for a person to work to achieve success.
2. Find a job within such an organisation where you can clearly identify the job goals so that performance in the role is clearly and unambiguously measurable.
3. Be very focused on managing your time.

   • Only attend functions (evening, lunch) where there is a direct business benefit. Too many business people accept all invitations because there 'may' be some benefit. Evaluate each invitation thoroughly.
   • Do not book meetings that start before 8.30 a.m. or start after 5 p.m. In this way you can still be home in time to tuck your kids into bed and in some way participate in their day.

- Don't do lunch meetings. If someone wants a meeting then do it over a cup of coffee in your or his or her office. This is a much more efficient use of your time.
- Don't attend meetings unless the outcome of the meeting will affect your area of responsibility and the participants of the meeting have the power to make changes.
- Avoid having status meetings (i.e. where the objective is just to chat and update everybody). Use email as an effective mechanism for updating status.
- Mark in your diary as immutable appointments all school concerts, performances and other such functions.
- Attend your children's school or schools at least for half a morning once a term for each child. Do canteen duty, reading class or help out in PE. Don't change these time commitments. If this time has to come out of your holidays then still book the time with your children at their school.
- Avoid taking work home if at all possible. Look carefully at what you are tempted to take home and first decide if the world will collapse if it waits until the following week.
- Plan your future financial needs. Work out how much you really need to live and keep to that plan as opposed to working to develop larger and larger piles of cash that will sit in the bank when you die.

WRAPPING UP

I understand that many people will not be able to implement some of these suggestions. If you do nothing else, then just make sure you spend regular time with your children at night and weekends and get to their school at least once a term. By staying connected at this level you will at least be reminded of what you are missing. Perhaps this will then motivate you to try to find other small ways to become more connected with your children on a day-to-day basis. It sounds simplistic, but the truth is your children grow up fast. When I look at our eldest daughter, I am torn between my joy at the fact she is embarking on her own journey and my sadness at the fact that she will spend less time with my wife and I as she builds her own life. My only consolation is that I feel I have enjoyed as much time with her as possible.

4

Involved fathering

Deciding to have a child is arguably the most important decision of your life. Once committed that's it. You are a father for the rest of your life. Through good times and bad, through employment and unemployment, through marriage and divorce, you never lose the responsibility of fatherhood.

The majority of fathers I know are similarly affected by the birth of their child. They share the same level of love and commitment to their new baby, the same sense of wonderment at what has just transpired and the effect on their lives. They are, to a man, changed individuals.

All fathers start on an equal footing. They have the same relationship with their new children as any other father. Yet each father will take a different road forward in terms of his approach to fathering.

It would be profoundly incorrect to attempt to judge one approach to fathering as right and another as wrong. But there is one characteristic of the father-child relationship which I believe provides both for happier children and happier fathers.

PROVIDER MORE THAN PROTECTOR

The most common definition of the role of the father is that of provider and protector. However, as we approach the 21st century the provider aspect seems to be dominant. As a description of the modern father it seems almost perfect. What more can he do than provide for his family? Going forth and hunting down food for the family, returning late at night to the renovated Federation cave (again a function of the father's work efforts). As the ravenous family devours the fresh supply of game the father can reflect on the completion of another good day's labour for his flesh and blood.

This idea of the primary role of the father as a provider is not in itself misguided. It's the narrow use of the term that is in fact the issue.

NOT BY BREAD ALONE

In many households where finances are very tight the father's income must necessarily be the main support for the family. Without this primary income source the family would no longer be able to maintain its basic standard of living. In such cases it is tempting to regard the provision of money as the defining characteristic of fatherhood.

Yet I would prefer a broader definition. While a provider in the parental sense is one who supplies the means of support for his or her family, surely such support should be more than just financial and include the provision of advice, comfort, affection, wisdom and empathy as well as money. Each of these activities requires effort on behalf of the provider and none is singularly more important than any other.

Thus the ideal providers, either fathers or mothers, are those who give their families both financial and emotional support. It doesn't matter which partner takes the main responsibility of being the family breadwinner, though this is something which the male-dominated executive corps of Australian business find it extremely difficult to accept.

Equally, if it happens that either partner is spending an inordinate amount of time earning money, at the expense of providing for the family in other ways, then ideally the latter should take precedence, even though this may mean a significant drop in disposable household income. Such a trade-off, however, not only requires careful planning but also challenges the accepted behaviour of Australian executives.

A Reborn Dad

A friend of mine found that he had a lot of time on his hands. He runs his own consulting company and days before the start of an agreed contract the client reneged on the agreement. It took him several weeks to obtain some new business to replace the lost contract. Watching him during this period was very interesting on a number of scores.

Most interesting was the way he dealt with the problem of being the 'provider' and also how he utilised the extra time on his hands to develop a deeper level of understanding of his pre-school age daughter.

When he initially lost the contract and the prospective income it represented he felt very low. He often told me he felt that because he was not bringing in any money he was failing as a father and specifically as the provider for his family.

I told him he needed to broaden his definition of being a provider. While it naturally included bringing home the money which allowed a family to function, that was only part of the story. It also meant providing them with love, attention, empathy, respect and time. A family environment that helped children grow up stable, secure, happy and loving was a result more of the time and attention of the parents than the size of the father's salary.

The only way to be a 'provider' in this broader sense required time with one's family, I said. Nothing could replace time with children as a method of developing a deeper understanding of their lives and their needs as they grew up. Given the time he had to spare until a new contract came up, I therefore suggested he spend some of it in this way with his family.

He had previously heard me talking about taking reading classes and doing canteen shifts at school, but had always been too busy to think seriously about what I was saying. One day, however, he decided to go to his daughter's pre-school and take part in reading a story to her class.

'I was very very nervous walking into the classroom and being confronted by the group of three-year-olds,' he told me afterwards. 'I looked across to see Paige and I could see just how proud she was to have her daddy there at school so I continued on. It was such a great day for both of us, I'm going to make sure I do it on a regular basis.'

He also helped out with a school excursion with some other parents and again he told me what a wonderful time he had, listening to the children tell stories and ask questions. He felt he was part of a special occasion and

was only sorry so few other fathers were there to experience it.

In due course he won a major consulting contract and went back to his customary busy week. But he still makes time to undertake activities at his daughter's school for her benefit—and also his own.

INVOLVEMENT: THE WAY TO GO

Rather than seeing the father's role merely as a provider, materially or emotionally, I prefer to think of it in terms of being involved or not with children. Although 'involved fatherhood', as I like to call it, assumes that most fathers will automatically carry out their responsibilities to look after their children—and in my view those who do not should be penalised severely for their neglect—it goes much further than that.

- Involved fathering means that the corporate father constantly plans his business life so as to maximise the opportunity to spend time with his children, not only 'playing' with them but learning about their lives firsthand, not just at home but elsewhere.
- Involved fathering means prioritising time with your children in relation to work commitments.
- Involved fathering also means giving the same degree of thought to learning about your children's lives and interests as you would to a business problem. Some fathers I know make great efforts to understand the economy and the state of the market for business investments, but somehow can't adopt the same approach to their children.

Down on the Farm–
Without Dad

Some years ago my wife and I took our children to a farm holiday near Picton, NSW. The usual mixed group of people was there—mostly families with fathers, mothers and children, but also some mothers by themselves with their children. As I observed the other people I could not help thinking about what their lives were like and how they took to the issue of involved parenting.

One particular woman who was there with her two young sons interested me. She was very well dressed, wearing loads of jewellery and yet with a sullen look about her. But one day my wife got talking to her. She said that my wife was lucky that I was there for the holiday, as she herself had long ago stopped asking her husband to come on holidays because he had said no so many times. He worked six days a week, then sailed all day Sunday and to add insult to injury was even planning to take a month off to go sailing. The woman's sullen expression was the result of a life of much sadness and disappointment. She could see—as could everyone at the farm stay—that her boys desperately needed him to be with them and yet she had long since learned that her husband was not 'that type of father'.

I am not suggesting that a father—or mother—does not deserve to have a holiday away from the family. People need time away. My point is that this father was allocating no time to be a father. He was providing for the family in a material way but he was not providing for them in any other ways. He lived a wonderful life (in

materialistic terms) in the affluent Sydney suburb of Mosman, with the children attending a private school. He was clearly successful in business but he was failing terribly as a husband and a father.

I am certainly not suggesting that fathers should snoop and spy on their children in such a way as to smother their efforts to develop their own independent existence. This process is very important for a child. But if a father wants to be a useful adviser to his children when they are seeking guidance then he needs to understand the total environment they inhabit. The home environment is only part of this. As children grow up the 'away from home' aspects of their lives take on more importance. Thus for a father to be able to provide sound and relevant advice, he needs to understand what that side of their experience is all about.

BACK TO SCHOOL TIME

All parents ask their children about their day at school but unless they're familiar with the school routine and its physical layout, as well as knowing their children's teachers and some of their classmates and friends, then they won't really understand what that day was like.

In the business world, where a manager is in charge of remote branches, it goes without saying that he won't be able to understand exactly how well they're operating unless he visits them personally as often as possible, notwithstanding all the daily phone calls and weekly or monthly written reports. Moreover, such visits usually occur during a normal business day. It's no use going to a staff social function at night or on a weekend if you want to get some idea of the daily flow of business at the branch.

The same applies to understanding your children's school. If you really want to understand the context of the stories they tell you about school, you need to have some first hand knowledge of what it's like. Who is this strict Mr Smith who never lets them talk out of turn? How far away are the lockers from the classroom? Why does the bell after lunch always go earlier on Wednesday afternoons than other days?

I often meet fathers who seem to believe they have a good understanding of their children's school environment and yet the only time they ever go there is for some formal function or for weekend clean-up work. While both these types of events are important for children (and fathers), they are no substitute for the wealth of information you can gather by attending a normal school day and helping with reading or taking on canteen work or some other activity.

WITH A SPRING IN MY STEP

I have found that I learn a lot about my children's school life by carrying out tasks at the school where I am able to watch the normal daily ritual and see how they interact with others, both as individuals and in groups, and how the teachers work with the children. This is very different to being one of thirty parents attending a specially arranged 'school function' where the children are too conscious of the group of parents in attendance to behave spontaneously.

When I leave the school after being involved with the children, I always go with a spring in my step. There is something wonderfully uplifting about spending time with children, watching them learn, watching them play and being part of their day, not to mention the sheer pleasure of seeing their happy, smiling faces. Heading off to work after a morning spent at school also helps me keep my perspectives clear. I know that I have added something to a group of children and as a result I can better judge my own work activities. It is often easier to handle office problems with the clear sense of balance that a school morning provides.

Why then is it so unusual to find fathers involved in school activities? Many mothers take part in them and become closer to their children as a result. There is no evidence that fathers love their children any less than mothers do. So why is there such a difference in their level of involvement?

In their study 'Facilitating future changes in men's family roles', J.H. Pleck, M.E. Lamb and J.A. Levine proposed a way of understanding how the characteristics of a father's job affect his involvement with his children.

There were four main factors which were found to determine a father's interaction with his child: motivation, skills, social supports, and institutional barriers. A father's motivation is driven from a sense of compensating for the inadequacies of his own father, or his wife's employment; a mid-life reassessment; or from a cultural reinforcement of the role of fathers in society. Skills refer to whether the father has confidence in his ability to be more involved with his children, while social support includes emotional encouragement from partners and peers. Institutional barriers are set in place by employers in their workplace practices and policies for the provision of leave for fathers.

The study found that a one-hour reduction in the working week was more likely to lead to the father spending the hour as leisure time rather than as an hour devoted to interaction with his child. The evidence showed that while workplace education and support programs provided some fathers with the skills and encouragement for greater interaction with their children, a greater provision of workplace innovations would not, on its own, increase the level of the father's involvement.

OLD HABITS DIE HARD

Without the influence of a wake-up call or mid-life crisis very few fathers are motivated to modify significantly the amount of time spent with their children, let alone allocating more of the working week to time with their children at school or similar environments. In the executive business world that I know there exists only a very low level of motivation to change the status quo.

Combined with this is a lack of social support. Unfortunately the idea of an executive re-arranging his work schedules to attend a pre-school reading assistance program or somesuch has not yet caught on very widely. It is also unlikely that an executive would be able to suggest that a weekly management meeting be re-scheduled to allow him to carry out canteen duty. While I suspect that many fathers would wish that more of their work colleagues felt as they do, the silence that surrounds this issue ensures that nothing will change.

Executives also face substantial institutional barriers preventing them from fulfilling their responsibilities as fathers, not so much in the shape of formal work policies as 'expected behaviour' in a corporate environment. It is quite acceptable for an executive to have to dramatically change their schedule to attend an 'important' business meeting. But sickness of a family member appears to be one of the few acceptable personal reasons for changing one's work schedule. As yet there remains an attitude that 'time to attend school' is not worth discussion, let alone being acceptable.

Such barriers are all about being seen to be committed and this translates to being seen to put in the hours and make the company the absolute priority. Often this 'work first' mantra comes from the managing director. My experience has shown that the majority of managing directors have developed their careers in an environment which can only be classed as family unfriendly. This has led to their having had to trade off time with their family for career advancement. Finally they make it as MD, but with their children now gone they seem to lack any memory of the trauma caused to their family life by the time requirements of their climb to the top. Further, they seem unable to think in terms of developing a working environment for their younger executives which is conducive to a healthy family life.

It is as though there is a sense of 'I survived and so will you' in the mentality of many senior executives in this country. The fact that they should be applying the same ethic with regard to family involvement that existed in the 1950s and 60s to today shows just how backward and negative their attitudes are.

I find many younger and more enlightened executives have a desire to be more involved with their children and yet they're only prepared to talk about it in private, well away from their employer or manager. My hope is that as these younger executives reach senior roles they will remember the turmoil they went through in trying to be involved fathers while pursuing their careers. Perhaps then we will see significant attitudinal changes in corporate Australia.

Of course the reverse may also occur. By the time these men reach senior roles they too may have become products of their environment. They will no longer recall the passion they had for their families and all they will remember is that they survived (nearly) without devoting much time to their families. Such a scenario would subject yet another generation of Australian business leaders to a poor father-child relationship and all the problems for both sides that result.

FATHERS' CANTEEN: A CASE STUDY

1. DOING THE FRUIT

When we first arrived back in Australia I had a strong desire to be an involved father and to really try to understand the environments my children would be thrust into. Thus in the early days of my first daughter attending pre-school I elected to do the 'fruit' one morning a term while also dropping her at school every morning.

'Doing the fruit' required me to be at pre-school at 9 a.m. and stay until approximately 11.30 cutting up fruit for the children's playtime break, then cleaning up afterwards.

I was the first father ever to take on this task, as up to then fathers' involvement had been limited to weekend working bees and being on the pre-school committees (real men activities!).

At first I was very apprehensive. My motivation was strong but I had little support either from other fathers or my work colleagues (this was not something that was on the agenda at monthly management meetings). I definitely had to overcome some institutional barriers. Then I scheduled the time in my diary as if it was an important meeting with a client. I knew I had to make sure I got there, otherwise the other person rostered—a mother—would have to do all the work. I couldn't let her or the children down.

I drove my daughter to the pre-school that morning and waited around as most of the mothers and fathers did. Then all the other parents went off, leaving my canteen co-worker and me with the teachers and the children. For the first forty-five minutes or so we were able to join in activities with the children and I noticed how different they were when there were few adults around. They were more open and also interacted more with each other, including some children who had been clinging to their parents' clothes when they were being dropped off. It occurred to me that I was experiencing a very treasured moment. It was as though I had been given access to something that was both wonderful and yet limited to only a few parents.

My co-worker and I then went and started preparing the fruit. My daughter was allowed to come and chat to me from time to time. Her attitude was quite interesting. She was clearly chuffed that her father was at school not only because it was me but because dads had never done fruit before. I was surprised how enjoyable I found it.

After each morning I would leave and go to work and always felt very special and very content with life. It was as though time with the children was like time spent at the fountain of youth.

Following my first 'fruit' morning I was so excited that I started to tell parents about this wonderful experience. A couple of the fathers seemed to understand what I meant, but most of them just heard me out politely. It was clear they thought I had somehow 'lost it' and there was no way they would be caught out in a pre-school kitchen cutting fruit—this was not a thing that men do.

2. TACKLING THE TUCKSHOP

I continued to do fruit at pre-school until, two years later, my eldest daughter started kindergarten and I decided to upgrade my activity—to the school canteen.

It seemed logical that since I had enjoyed myself so much at pre-school, working at the primary school canteen would be even better. So I duly put my name down on the roster to do canteen duty once a term. But when the roster came back my wife's name had replaced mine. It turned out the people in charge thought I had meant to put my own name on some other list and not the canteen roster. Again, not men's work, you see.

As with the pre-school fruit, I approached my first canteen day with some trepidation. I was on with three mothers and they were all experienced hands. I felt distinctly out of place.

But my worries evaporated when the school was let out

for morning recess. It was a lot of fun serving the children, then making the lunches and delivering them in baskets to the classrooms. I was not exactly solving the problem of Third World hunger, but I felt I was doing something of value to the children and to myself.

Most fun were the little kindergarten kids who would come up to the counter and order two packets of carob buds, one apricot log, a packet of popcorn and an iceblock and then proceed to give me 20c to pay for it all. I ended up paying for the shortfall on many kindergarteners' recess orders as I felt it was too soon to introduce these five-year-olds to the concept of 'You don't have enough money'. That could wait for first grade.

I was puzzled at first when some of the women helpers would ask why I volunteered for canteen duty. I would explain that I felt it was a way to see children in another light, as well as to understand more about how the school functioned during the day. The response I received was always the same: 'You're lucky your job allows you to do this.'

It was only some months later I realised this really translated as: 'You don't have an important job because men with important jobs could not take time off for canteen.' At the time I was Microsoft director for Southeast Asia as well as the director for Advanced Technology. By any standard I had a very senior and important job, one that was extremely demanding in time and energy. The difference between my position and that of these women's husbands was that their husbands had *chosen* not to participate in their children's lives to the same extent as I had.

I did point out to some of these women that it was strange that quite a few of their husbands with important jobs were somehow able to attend golf days, race days, football matches and the like, and yet could not take three hours out every four months to be involved in a school activity.

3. DADS' ARMY

After my first year of canteen duty I decided to organise a fathers' roster. It wasn't that I was uncomfortable working with the mothers, but that I wanted to help other fathers experience the pleasure and excitement I was having.

It was difficult to get four men to agree to come on the first fathers' canteen, but it was a day to remember.

The others were as apprehensive as I had been and a couple were not sure if they were up to it. The wife of one of them—the managing director of a large, successful Australian computer company—called me to say that she thought her husband was going to be a disaster on the day.

However, the group performed well and they all seemed to enjoy themselves. When recess came around they tended to stand back from the counter at first, but within a few minutes they were caught up in the fun of serving the kids. Later a couple of them went out into the playground to play handball with some of the children and immediately found themselves surrounded by a large crowd of youngsters, cheering and laughing. Many of them went up to the men, wanting to talk or play, as if they were starved for adult male attention.

At the morning's end all four men told me what a wonderful time they had had and asked to be rostered on again. Two of them in particular, who had at first appeared to be quite nervous and uncomfortable but ended up being as involved as the others, both said emphatically that this had been 'one of the best days of my life'.

But what was so special about it? It was not as though we had just climbed Everest with no oxygen tanks and in our Speedos. What had happened was that four fathers had experienced an activity involving children which had touched them deep inside. For a brief time they had seen their kids in a very different light and themselves as well. They had done something which provided them with great joy and a sense of fulfilment as well as providing their children (and the school population generally) with an equally fulfilling experience.

Some people with whom I have discussed this experience have attempted to trivialise it. 'What's the big deal in making a bunch of sandwiches?' I am often asked. My response is quite consistent. 'Come and do canteen one morning and then tell me if it is a big deal or not.' Interestingly, many fathers baulk at the challenge. Clearly they love their children, but the stigma attached to taking time off work to do school canteen duty is too much for many of them to overcome.

I have since organised many more groups of fathers and as with the first lot they have all had a great time and want to be asked back. I have been running Dad's Tuckshop at my daughters' new school for eight years. Over fifty fathers volunteer to take part each year and more than fifty per cent come back the next year. It is also pleasing to note that Dad's Tuckshop at my daughters' old school continues to run along happily, giving fathers an opportunity to engage with their sons and daughters on the school campus and have some fun.

SOME LESSONS TO BE DRAWN

This small experience in getting fathers more involved in the daily school routine has taught me a few things.

Firstly, children obviously loved having their fathers, or any fathers, involved in the school activities. They were used to having mothers come and help out, but it was quite unique for fathers to take part.

Secondly, the fathers themselves all had a wonderful experience. They were each able to extract themselves from the daily grind of their work schedule to enjoy seeing their children—and other people's as well—in a typical day's school situation.

Thirdly, the relative success of the venture was due to the fact that the fathers realised that it was a beneficial and valuable exercise which not only strengthened their bonds with their own children but earned them the respect and gratitude of the teachers and other parents. It also gave them a far better understanding of the school environment.

I suspect that the fathers who did attend also had to overcome their own set of institutional barriers and lack of peer support at work. From the response they received on canteen day I can only assume it was worth the effort.

While it may be said that until then the fathers had chosen not to become involved in school activities, this is more an example of a choice by default. By allowing their normal work routine and peer expectation to rule their schedule, they did not consciously decide not to take part in things. It was more a case of their not being clear that they had such a choice. It is not as if they had been regularly asked by their children to come to school and undertake activities and they had refused. In any case children don't make such requests because they don't expect it of their fathers. Conversely, fathers don't think about being involved because it is outside their frame of reference.

But unless they do start to think about it, they'll never know what they're missing. Both children and fathers get so much from such activities together that no-one can afford not to take part in them. After all, children are at school for only a few years and to let this period go by without making the most of it is a great opportunity lost forever.

The Teen Years

Parents of older children give you that look. You can see in their eyes the journey they have been on, from dramatic exits from out-of-control parties, to seeing their home decimated by a 'gathering', to horror at the choice of outfit their teenage daughter chooses to wear out. When they ask what age your eldest child is and you give an answer with a number less than fifteen they give you an 'oh you just wait ...' look that sends shivers down your spine.

If you can get them to be expansive, you hear stories of teenage drinking, parents condoning the sexual relationship between their fifteen-year-old daughter and her nineteen-year-old boyfriend, and boys who disappear to places unknown on a Saturday night.

I am told that by the time kids turn nineteen they have usually worked out that binge drinking is actually pretty stupid, as is smoking and doing drugs. It seems, however, that at fifteen all of these activities hold fascination for a growing number of teenagers.

It was into this cauldron that my wife and I launched

ourselves when our eldest daughter turned fifteen. What I can relay is that all of the items mentioned above do occur, but with less frequency than expected. More interestingly, there seems to be a correlation between the relationship of a child and their parents and the degree to which they go off the edge.

There are, of course, parents who have deep and loving relationships with their children and the children still go wild. Yet my experience is that if there is not a strong and mutually caring relationship between the parent and the child then there is a reasonable chance that things will spin out of control during this difficult period.

It is easy to talk about independence, trust, self-development and finding your way. The reality is that teenage children need to have observant and concerned parents helping them navigate this part of life's journey. Of course they need greater independence at fourteen than ten, but they still need boundaries and parents need to ensure their child is not thrust into any situation they might not be able to handle.

THE ESSENCE OF INVOLVED FATHERING

There's more to being a decent father, of course, than turning up at school every so often to cut fruit or prepare lunches. Involved fathering can take many forms and comprises a wide range of emotions and responses.

Firstly, it means you have to change your priorities. You accept that work is the key to your life as regards both financial security and self-esteem, but you need to be able to determine which are your really important work com-mitments and which ones are not. Once you have got this clear in your mind you can start to reschedule your life accordingly.

Secondly, you have to be prepared to allocate more time to your children than the customary thirty minutes or so each night and a few hours on weekends. You need to spend time with them when they are involved in their daily routine, such as school, sport and other activities, as well as going on excursions with them as a parent helper or taking part in other school functions. Children are very different at night from the way they are during the day or at weekends, and to really understand your children you need to give up part of your day to be part of theirs.

Thirdly, involved fathering means moving out of your comfort zone—letting your heart take you where you want to go and not letting peer or work values dictate how you want to interact with your children. Business executives who do not get close to their children are the ones who end up lonely, pathetic men and once they have retired seem to lose the very fibre of their existence. Don't let it happen to you.

Finally, it means realising that time with your children is as important to their development as time spent with their mother. Children need the love, comfort and support of their fathers as much as their mothers'. Moreover, your emotional development and stability depend to a great extent on your being able to spend lots of time with your children.

WRAPPING UP

I n the spirit of our quick-fix era, outlined below are a few things you should undertake today if you want to be an involved father and reap the benefits for your children and yourself that will result:

- Spend at least one morning a term at your children's school involved in an activity where there are very few parents and you interact a lot with the children.
- Find out what your children think about a range of topics which are important to them (not you) and see where you stand on these issues.
- Find out whom your children see as heroes/heroines and why.
- Find out about your children's friends and what they think of them, as well as what you think of them.
- Find out first-hand about your children's teachers by being involved at school and getting to know them.
- Start discussing your ideas about fathering with your work colleagues.

5

Fathers and corporate life

We are not hapless beings caught in the grip of forces we can do little about. Organisation has been made by man; it can be changed by man. The fault is not in the organisation; in short, it is in our worship of it.

William H. Whyte, Jr, The Organisation Man

The idea of a father being away from the family for a significant part of every day is a relatively new phenomenon. Prior to the industrial age most fathers spent their time working their land, constantly in the company of their family. Of course, their 'working week' was much longer even than what is considered a long week today (over fifty hours). Yet the father was basically close at hand and the children were able to be with their father (and mother) for most of the day, learning the ways of the land.

With the Industrial Revolution people were forced off the land and into the cities, where men took jobs in the new factories and other enterprises which were springing up, while the women stayed home to take care of the children and run the house.

Thus the concept of father as the provider and mother as the homemaker began to take shape. Both men and women were assumed to have been rewarded by their respective roles—although no-one ever asked if they actually felt rewarded. Little thought was given to the effect such a profound social change would have on the families of the workers concerned, particularly on the relationship between father and child.

MAN THE MASTER—OR SLAVE TO HIS WORK?

The role of work has continued to take on more importance in men's lives. In her book *The Time Bind*, Arlie Hochschild claims to have found that most men saw themselves primarily as wage earners, while the care of others was seen to be 'extra'. Even in situations where wives also work there has not necessarily been a change in attitude by their husbands. Hochschild observed, in the corporation she was researching, that a third of husbands did more work around the house as a result of the wife also going out to work. But another third hadn't changed at all and the remainder actually did less work around the house.

The office has become as much a part of life as the home. In many instances the office now defines the family life well beyond the impact of the wages earned to support the family. The time spent by men away from home at work means that they have less of a chance to understand or interact with their children. Among men at executive level I have noticed a greater degree of work domination than with the general office worker. Their lives tend to be almost completely defined by their work commitments.

The pace of change brought about by increasing global competition has made many business careers much more tenuous and demanding. Combined with this is the sense that the job is never done. No matter what stage a particular business transaction is at, there is always more to do in terms of developing new contacts, re-establishing relationships with past clients, reorganising and restructuring internal divisions and groups and keeping abreast of worldwide developments of competitors. There never seems to be an indicator of when 'the job is done'. Holidays become minor rest points between major investments of time and energy in career and business development. Family time has become time to rest between corporate battles or, worse, time to catch up on reading and office work and yet the magic of their child's development slips past without much noise.

The Peripheral Family

Home and family life appear to have become peripheral activities to the central role of work, especially in top management. Recently, while undertaking consultancy work, I have been asking senior executives I know about their priorities.

In all cases they respond that their family is the most important 'thing' in their lives. Sounds wonderful. Yet

what does this really mean? Then I ask the next set of questions:

Q. How many hours do you work on average per week?

A. More than sixty.

Q. How often do you have late-night functions or meetings?

A. Two-three times a week.

Q. How often do you travel for work?

A. One week a month.

Q. How often do you take work home?

A. Most weekends.

And still they say the family is the most important 'thing' in their lives!

An English couple, J.M. and R.E. Paul, studied the relationship between career and home life of eighty-six managers and their wives. They observed that the typical manager viewed his family as the most important aspect of his life, but he obtained his greatest sense of achievement and mastery from his work rather than through building a family or his leisure life.

THE COMMUNITY OF THE JOB

According to R.S. Weiss, in his book *Staying the Course*, men appear to require association to sustain themselves. Membership in a valued community is a key association. Often this is the community of work and men experience severe distress where they have lost membership of such a group. In many ways the work environment provides not only the financial support for a man and his family but also the social environment which feeds and nurtures a man's self esteem.

Men's definition of themselves is often determined by their work and career. Work provides them with the base from which to establish a career through contacts that could not be obtained in a normal social setting. Through work functions men can meet up with influential business and political leaders, people who ordinarily would be uncontactable if it were not for their work or company function. Work often provides support in the form of 'the company'. If the company is well known and successful and the man has an important job in it, doors open. Without 'the company' opportunities and contacts are far less easy to obtain. The offices of many men in senior business positions I visit are also much better appointed than their homes. More facilities, resources on tap to get 'things' done, state-of-the-art computers, million-dollar views and expensive furnishings.

For many executive men work has become the way they want to be seen and to be recognised. Introductions quickly establish one's position and company as a way of ensuring that the work persona is clearly recognised. Even social events quickly take on a work approach as work-focused men congregate with men who come from similar business environments (so they can talk shop), in situations where social discourse may provide an opening for future business arrangements.

Work as a determining factor of life and the overflow from work to non-work life is prevalent in the case of executives where many have lost their individual sense of purpose and are now in all ways extensions of their job title and their companies.

Those senior executives who say the family is the most important 'thing' in their life have a conflict between what gives them a sense of achievement (more often than not work) and how they feel they should respond. It is not that these men do not love their children or that in a time of crisis they would not rush to their aid. Yet life is usually not about dramatic crises demanding immediate action. In a society where the majority of people may never face a 'crisis' situation, it is easy to say 'Of course, if something was wrong I would drop everything and be there for my child or my wife.' Life is more often about day-to-day events that shape the development of the child (and for that matter the relationship between father and child). The increasing degree in which the work environment provides the temptation for men to spend less time with their family is a problem for society as a whole.

WORK VERSUS FAMILY—FAMILY VERSUS WORK

There is a wide body of literature on the concept of work/family and family/work conflict. Generally it has been found that family or private life concerns rarely interfere with work. However, work concerns pervade family and leisure lives. Two-thirds of men admit they wind down slowly from work and then spend a considerable amount of family and leisure time thinking about work issues.

A study conducted by Bartolome and Evans found that only one in four male managers saw the weekend as a time to leave work behind and devote themselves to personal and family interests. The 'job' had taken a strangle hold on executive men's lives. Their priorities were centred on being effective at work and then using their remaining energy and resources to tackle family and personal interests. One manager in the Bartolome-Evans survey noted: 'If I'm miserable on the job, I'll be miserable at home. The converse would not be true.'

Others said that even though their families were the most important things in their lives, they had their most satisfying experiences at work. While they professed a deep love for their wives and children, they also conceded that they did not spend enough time with them.

Bartolome and Evans also found that managers coped with the ambivalence that was inherent in their lifestyles by limiting their focus of attention and concern to one of a few parts of their lives at a particular stage. This life-stage theory indicated that managers in their late twenties to early thirties were focused on launching their careers. The group in their mid-thirties to early forties was marked by a turning towards private concerns, with more of them starting to reflect more deeply on life. The third stage, from the early forties to the fifties, was characterised by an integration of personal and professional life or by a resignation to a more fragmented lifestyle.

Graeme Russell and Gillian Savage from Macquarie University and Kevin Durkin from the University of Western Australia conducted a survey on attitudes to work/family balance. Ten per cent of female respondents indicated that they felt they had compromised child rearing and family life for their jobs or careers, compared with twenty per cent of men who felt the same way. To the reverse proposition, forty per cent of women said they felt that they had compromised their careers for their family life, compared with just fifteen per cent of men. By contrast, a study undertaken by Adrienne Burgess of the Institute of Public Policy Research in Britain found that three out of four men believed that their family relationships had been damaged by their working lives.

In a study published in Jane Hood's book *Men, Work and Family*, Beth Willinger researched changing attitudes of a group of university students from 1980 to 1990. Interestingly, one question dealt with the issue of how the person would respond to an impending but undesirable promotion to executive level. Significantly more men in 1990 (36.6 per cent) than in 1980 (27.6 per cent) would accept the promotion, because they could neither 'resist the urge to move upward nor live with a reputation as a guy headed nowhere'.

Further, Willinger found that while there had been a significant trend in the past decade for men to recognise the legitimacy of both women's employment and men's family work, men remained reluctant to accept the kind of restructuring that would enable men and women to participate equally in both work and family roles.

Professor Craig Littler from the University of Southern Queensland found that the Australian male career was now likely to entail a working life of sixty hours per week for fifty weeks a year. This surely does not leave much time for the father to be a true participant in his children's lives. Research in the U.S. indicates that the increased time spent at work by American male executives meant that on average even though they will retire at the same age as their fathers they will in fact have worked up to ten years longer. This is due to the ever-lengthening working week.

As noted earlier in *The Time Bind*, Arlie Hoschchild noted that the employee handbook described a list of unofficial norms and their corresponding career implications. 'Time spent on the job is an indication of commitment.

Work more hours' was one gem. Another was, 'More hours indicates you are paying your dues.'

WORK AND FAMILY: THE MICROSOFT EXPERIENCE

My business experience conforms to the literature. It seems that in most businesses there is an expectation that the working week can now routinely take up not only twelve or fourteen hours a day during the week but also time over the weekend. I remember being caught up in the game of being in the office early and leaving late as though time spent on the job was in itself a major achievement. Managers fostered this culture of 'dedication' by regularly calling both early morning (before 8 a.m.) and late afternoon (after 5 p.m.) meetings and expecting everyone to attend.

Microsoft Part 2

At Microsoft headquarters in Seattle the atmosphere was perhaps even worse. Weekend work was never asked for but always expected. There was a sense that the whole week (7x24 hours) was available Microsoft time and that if the work demanded more time then the employee should give it. The most disturbing aspect of this type of environment was that employees happily turned up to work the long days and weekends with little concern. Their families were not always as accomodating but in the end the company won by ensuring its employees were 'rewarded' in material terms and by providing exciting challenges for them to work on.

The combination of good working conditions, exciting challenges to work on and great employee benefits naturally promoted the concept that work dedication was a good thing. On many occasions I would arrive at work to find some employees in my development group fast asleep in sleeping bags under their desks proud of the fact that they only needed a few hours' sleep before embarking on the next day's programming challenge. Many of these people were quite well-off, living in very nice houses in beautiful parts of Seattle—not struggling students who couldn't afford to rent an apartment. They were just living a life that was seen as normal and expected.

Meetings would be regularly called on weekends. Again, no-one has a problem with work taking up time on the weekend when there is a crisis, but it seemed quite strange that normal product status meetings had to be held on the weekend. Bill Gates in his early days at Microsoft was known for his ability to be a six-hour turnaround man—i.e. from the time he left work on one day until the time he arrived for work on the next only six hours had passed.

WHEN HOME BECOMES AN OFFICE EXTENSION

What I noticed was that Microsoft had perfected a process that is now becoming quite widespread across both the U.S. and Australia. Microsoft had effectively blurred the line between the workplace and the home to the point that work had actually invaded the home and home had become merely an extension of the work environment. In Microsoft's case this invasion was not something maliciously planned and executed. It was simply the result of a combination of executive expectations and the company's solicitous care of its employees.

The starting point was an executive team which had decided work really was the most important thing in their lives. They were consciously devoting sixty or seventy hours a week to it, combined with a work-dominated social calendar and a travel schedule that took them away from home for up to two weeks a month. They had become entranced by the challenge of changing the world through software. They knew that if Microsoft was not smart enough and did not execute fast enough then it would never reach its goals. Paranoia became a strong motivating force for the company. Every development schedule was too long and there was never enough time to get things done. The focus was on executing plans quickly and efficiently. In itself this desire to change the world was an admirable goal, but the road to financial success had an unfortunate effect on the time that fathers and mothers had with their children.

With Microsoft's managers leading by example it was not surprising that the whole of the company fell in behind this extreme work ethic.

The success of the company was truly due to the efforts of its staff. Microsoft developed software and this process is not about building large impenetrable physical assets but more about making your next software release better than what the next guy makes.

The Racehorse Company

The human resource managers at Microsoft were always focused, as was Bill Gates, on ensuring that the employees were treated well. The company provided the very best of health schemes, subsidised cafeterias (some open twenty-four hours to feed the workaholics, who numbered into the thousands), stock options (which turned many employees into millionaires after a few years' work), state-of-the-art computers to work on, high standards of office layout (everyone had his or her own office—everyone!), free soft drinks and of course lavish company social functions. Thus the situation developed where because the employees were treated incredibly well they were motivated to work harder, the company did better and the employees received more benefits and worked harder. Surely an example of success. Not quite.

I often referred to Microsoft as a racehorse company. Search out the best yearlings, feed them well, train them well, provide the best possible environment for them to perform well and focus the whole organisation on performance. This all works well when the employees are able to be treated in this manner. What happens when the racehorse doesn't want to race and train all the time? Answer: dog food. What happens when dedicated employees start to have children and these children need their parents around? In Microsoft's case the company never quite worked out how to respond to this dilemma.

DOUBTERS BEWARE

Initially people who started to question the company's work ethic were seen as no longer being committed. It was as though they had given up on religion. They had allowed another power (that of a love for their children) to take their focus away from the work of Microsoft. In an environment that was so obsessed by performance it seemed as though acting dedicated was as important as performing well.

More distressing was the response of many of the senior male employees I got to know during my time in Seattle. While I was still there I had begun to seriously question the work ethic not only in Microsoft but of all companies which were promoting this somewhat simplistic view of how to succeed. I remember having long conversations with several top executives about people being lousy fathers if they were to continue working the sort of hours that Microsoft expected.

Some of them tried to defend such practices by talking about 'quality time'. One particular vice-president told me how he ensured he was home by 8.30 p.m. so that he could have twenty minutes of 'quality' time with his children before they went to bed. I concluded that he must have had truly remarkable children—children who were able to store up all their stories of good and bad things that had happened during the day as well as their energy and sense of wonderment, all ready for their father to come home. My experience with children is that they are incredibly spontaneous and that when they first get home from school you get a flood of information about what happened, who said what to whom, what made them happy, sad, intimidated or strong. By late night this information flow slows to a trickle that can be summed up as a 'How was your day?—Fine' communication process.

What this man had done was to convince himself that he could in fact partake of the pleasures of the Microsoft work environment while also being a good father. The reality was that he was having a wonderful time at work but he was an absent father and husband. His kids had all the latest toys, went to the best schools, travelled to exotic places for holidays and yet they lacked the most important gift from their father. Time. Not quality time but quantities of time. Lots of it.

People like myself who continued to question Microsoft's family-unfriendly ways found themselves getting the cold shoulder. If you no longer believed that the job should be given the highest priority in your life but thought that children needed to have hours a day with their parents during their developing years, then you became quite an outsider.

TRYING TO KICK THE CORPORATE DRUG

The lure of the corporate environment can't be underestimated. While in the U.S. I knew of many very bright, caring men who were so caught up in the rush for career success and Microsoft executive recognition that they were missing out on their children's lives, as well as being oblivious to many problems their wives and children were having. The attraction of such an environment is very strong. It would not be too much to describe it in fact as an addiction.

Could the company have succeeded just as well if it had

been prepared to modify its culture? I definitely believed this was possible. While running Microsoft Australia I made it absolutely clear that I did not want people working late nights or weekends except in *real* emergency situations. I felt that if we could not do our jobs in a focused nine or ten hours a day then we were either incompetent or we were trying to do too much with too few resources. Microsoft Australia became one of the most successful subsidiaries around the world and Bill Gates often commented that he thought the morale at MS Australia was the best he had found anywhere in the Microsoft world.

I continued to believe that if you could focus people on the key tasks, remove time-wasting obstacles from their way and get them to work shorter days then you could in fact be very successful. Combined with this was my unfailing belief that if you worked fewer hours there was a chance that you were also going to be a better friend, father and husband and that your family would actually be more supportive of your employer.

I had tremendous support from my employees, as they felt they had found a manager who truly valued his family ahead of his job and yet was still focused on commercial success. Yet I was a lone voice in management circles.

THE GLOBAL VIRUS CATCHES ON

On returning to Australia in 1993 I hoped that the work obsession I had found at Microsoft was a peculiar characteristic of Microsoft or at least U.S. high technology companies. I expected to find back in Australia a business environment that was more accepting of the needs of children. This was not the case.

Throughout Australian big business I actually found the worst of both worlds. Not only were many businesses run by men who lacked any sense of vision of their companies or their industry, but moreover they did not have much of a view of their companies' place in this new world of global competition. Many of these men had also long ago lost any deep relationship with their wives and children. They had become parents during a time when the father was not expected to be around and when the mother was at home taking care of the home.

These same men had been trapped by a similar addiction to what I had found at Microsoft. While always saying their families came first, they spent by far the greater part of their energy on work. The culture of long work hours as a determinant of career success was alive and well in Australia. Not surprisingly, I found that most senior executives were not even prepared to discuss the question of 'lost fathering'.

Most distressing were my experiences with younger executives, those in their thirties and early forties. I half-expected the more crusty senior executives to not be open to the issues I wanted to discuss. But I also found that many younger executives were also unable to see the mistake they were making by not spending time with their children.

WORK FOR WORK'S SAKE

In a 1955 study reported by Weiss in *Staying the Course*, respondents were asked: 'If by some chance you inherited enough money to live comfortably without working, do you think that you would work anyway or not?' Eighty-two per cent said yes. With work so important to their wellbeing, and competent performance being so important to their place at work, men generally give work as much time and energy as it requires—and that can be a very great deal. They work because they want to and because they enjoy what work gives them. Money is only one benefit they receive from work.

Part of the reason is that work provides immediate or at least short-term feedback. You are rewarded or counselled, as the case may be, at least annually if not monthly on the financial performance of your area of responsibility. Work long hours on a tender and you can celebrate or commiserate on the result within a few weeks (or months)—a quick return on time invested. It seems as though business in general is focused on very short-term cycles. Even long-term business planning, undertaken to any significant degree by few companies in my experience, often looks only five years ahead.

Compare this with the long-term process of child development. Of course there is instant feedback: a baby's first smile, the first time your child calls you 'Daddy' or says 'I love you Daddy', the full-on hugs when you come home at night. Yet the endgame of childhood, the development of a happy, stable, loving, confident, active member of society takes many years. It can be argued that the job of fathering is never really done and so perhaps there is no end to the role, no point at which you can wash your hands of the task. The fact that the way a child turns out is the result of a combination of environment, heredity and parental and peer interaction means that no-one can guarantee delivery of a 'successful' child no matter how much care and attention are lavished on its development.

The 'I Turned Out OK' Myth

A friend of mine has a seventeen-year-old son and a twelve-year-old daughter and works in the finance industry as a director of a leading company. His division is expanding rapidly in what is a very competitive environment. He works long hours and often will spend seventy to eighty hours a week completing a tender. His wife does not work outside the home so he knows his children are well cared for. He takes his annual holidays with his family and always enjoys his time with them. He also takes an interest in his son's football and attends most games.

His work schedule means that he rarely sees his children during the week. Thus his interaction with his children is limited to weekends. While this is clearly better than none at all, a lot can happen between Monday and Friday that my friend misses out on. On many occasions I have tried to talk to him about the importance of spending as much time as possible with his children. His response is always more or less as follows:

'My father worked long hours and I turned out OK. Mary is at home so I know that David and Claire are being well taken care of. I don't need to see more of my children than I do. Besides, my work demands tremendous time commitments and I enjoy what I am doing.'

Even when I try to tell him how much he will get out of spending time with his children he falls back on the line that he did not need to see any more of his father and therefore neither do his children. As the years have rolled on the children have developed some disturbing behaviours. The son is very shut off and never talks to his parents. He is doing well at school but school counsellors are concerned that he does not seem to have close friends. The daughter seems more balanced, but while she is very close to her mother, she is dismissive of her father, stating that all she needs from him is money for clothes and mobile phones etc. My friend laughs all this off with 'they'll be fine'. They might be, but perhaps having a closer bond with them may have been beneficial to their development. I suspect the children are unlikely to be calling dad up in his retirement for a chat. The opportunity to create such a bond has gone.

The Shock of 'AHA'

John, a marketing executive, changed his view. For many years he has been building up a successful marketing company, the launch of which coincided with the birth of his first child. Starting a new business takes an immense amount of time and energy and the family was utterly dependent on its succeeding. He worked very long hours but was comforted by the fact that his child—and a subsequent sibling—had a mother at home, thus allowing him to concentrate on work.

When his first child was about five and the business was established, John found that although he was still working long hours he was enjoying what he was doing, as well as the fruits of his labour. He then had what I call an 'AHA' moment. One afternoon he came home from work early just as his son got home from kinder-garten. His son was very happy to see him, but when it came to playing the boy wanted to play with the kids next door. So he went in and played with the neigh-bouring kids—and their father. John's neighbour had a work schedule that allowed him to be home two or three afternoons a week and the boy wanted to play not just with the other kids but with him. He had developed a bond with the neighbour that in some ways was stronger than that with his father. This incident really shook John up. He suddenly realised that he was within a couple of years of never having the kind of relationship with his son that he had always wished for. He had not intentionally been neglectful but work had completely taken over him.

From that day forward he changed his work schedule. Nothing radical, but he made a point of being home for dinner three nights out of five and at least one afternoon a week. Since then he has developed a very strong rela-tionship with both his son and daughter and he now tells people how that afternoon years ago changed his life.

EXECUTIVE RULES. OK?

The most worrying development in Australian business in recent times is the way in which work is threatening to disrupt every aspect of people's lives. The continual threat of unemployment, even for senior executives and the sub-sequent loss of income—not to mention self-esteem—keep them focused on the job at hand. The result is a frenetic pace for executives in the work environment and a family life that at best accommodates the father's work schedule and at worst operates almost entirely without him.

It would be bad enough if this affected only senior exec-utives and their immediate families, but it also has a severe impact on the lives of many more people. Executives deter-mine an organisation's culture, establishing its ground rules and how it will work. By propagating certain values and acting in a particular way an executive will send a very clear message to ordinary employees. It will be obvious what is expected of them and what it takes to succeed.

In his book *Organisational Culture and Leadership*, E.H. Schein refers to the topic of how the culture of an organ-isation develops and how leaders shape an organisation's culture. The most powerful mechanisms for reinforcing the cultural values of a workplace were found to be: what leaders pay attention to, measure and control; leader reac-tions to critical incidents and organisational crisis; delib-erate teaching and coaching by leaders; criteria for allocation of rewards and status; and criteria for recruit-ment, selection, promotion, retirement and excommunica-tion. These mechanisms are subtle because they operate unconsciously in most organisations. Organisations tend to find attractive those candidates who resemble present members in style, assumptions and values. Once an organ-isation has evolved a mature culture through a long and rich history, that culture creates the pattern of perception, thought and feeling of every new generation in the organ-isation and therefore also causes it to be predisposed to certain kinds of leadership.

In that sense the organisational culture creates its own leaders, who create cultures which in turn create leaders.

Even in subtle ways an executive can establish the culture of a company. If a CEO establishes a regime of a

7.30 a.m. management meeting he is basically saying that if you want to be part of the senior management group you had better be prepared to be here early. A similar message goes out if the CEO regularly calls late afternoon meetings. By establishing weekend meetings the CEO is saying that all time is work time. Even if the CEO, after expecting employees to work many long nights and weekends, sends a group of employees and their spouses on a trip as a reward, he is really just enforcing the value of long work hours.

TWO CAUTIONARY TALES

1. THE MAN WHO THOUGHT A SICK CHILD MATTERED

Some years ago a friend of mine who was the technical director of a large computer company in Sydney told the managing director that he was taking the next day off as his son was not well and he had to stay home with him. The managing director exploded and the following Monday sent a note out to staff indicating that he expected all employees to put the company ahead of everything else in their lives and if anyone disagreed they should resign.

Nobody resigned as the recession was in full swing. What happened was that anyone who needed to look after a sick child or wanted to be with his or her children for some other valid reason had to think up an elaborate excuse to get time off.

When I told this story to a group of CEOs recently they all said how harsh and foolish the managing director had been. All agreed that a sick child should take priority over work (with the caveat that the sickness did not go on too long!). But when I asked whether they felt that attending an important function at a child's school was a justifiable reason to take time off the answer was no.

In essence, they were saying that other than for reasons of ill-health or some personal crisis a father's place was at work, not with his children. Fair enough, but they then went on to agree that business lunches and business golf or sport days were an important networking activity for managers aspiring to be business leaders. So it's quite all right to go out and play eighteen holes with a bunch of customers and suppliers in the hope that the game will generate business but it's not OK to take a small amount of work time off to visit a child at school.

2. THE MAN WHO THOUGHT HIS CHILDREN DIDN'T MATTER

Soon after arriving back from the U.S. I read an article in an Australian business magazine about a very successful Australian businessman who described how in the early years of his career he had been so focused on growing his business that he had not spent much time with his children. I was expecting him to say how bad he felt about this now and that he realised he had traded too much of his family's life for corporate success. He actually went on to say that while he had in fact not seen much of his kids for fifteen years, he had built a great company and the sacrifice was worth it. I then expected the journalist to make some slightly critical comment at least about this superficial view of the priorities of life.

Wrong again. The journalist continued reporting the

platitudes of this shallow man with not one suggestion that perhaps had he spent more time with his family he may have developed a better understanding of their lives and of his life.

I am sure that somewhere in Australia an impressionable young business person was reading this article, believing that to be a success he or she would need to make the same sort of compromise. An Australian business magazine continued to promote the great myth that success is singularly focused and measured in dollars alone. If it had really been concerned about developing better business managers in the future, it would have given some space to discussing other theories which defined success more broadly.

BREAKING THE FATHER-UNFRIENDLY CULTURE CYCLE

The combination of an entrenched corporate culture which is basically anti-family and the attitude of particular media outlets which continue to exalt the idea of 'work ethic = success' has resulted in fathers being no longer motivated to spend time with their children if it will in any way compromise their work performance. The accepted position that work must take priority over all other aspects of people's lives has been largely fostered by senior executives who in most cases have forgotten what it is like to have young children and have long since lost emotional contact with their families.

Research indicates that the conflict between work and family is greatest for male executives when they have small children. It is during this period, when the child goes to sleep early, that it more openly desires time with its father. Once the children are older a number of things occur. Firstly the child is more likely to be awake when the father returns from work, thus providing an opportunity for father-child communication on a daily basis. Secondly, and quite sadly, as children grow up they come to accept that their father is 'not around much'. Their initial feelings of sadness are now buried well below an accepting exterior.

Given that most senior executive and board positions are held by men with older children, it is not surprising to find that they are generally unsympathetic to the needs of fathers with young children. My conversations with many younger executives confirm that ideally they would like to spend more time with their children, but to express such sentiments publicly would have a detrimental effect on their careers. These men then struggle on, occasionally saying they have a doctor's appointment or a remote business meeting when they are in fact visiting their children's schools. However, by the time they reach senior management levels they have themselves become desensitised to the powerful feelings they had years ago and the cycle of father-unfriendly company culture continues.

The only way to break this cycle is for more men to say what they are feeling. Men who have young children and want to spend time with them should have the opportunity to do so. Senior executives should encourage fathers to be more involved in their children's lives as something which will help, not hinder, their careers. Younger executives should demand that performance counts and not whether they are 'playing the game'.

The shallowness of work-obsessed executives should be brought to public attention. Men who have achieved business success but have left behind a stream of broken families and under-fathered children should be exposed for what they really are: monodimensional people who do not have the wisdom or ability to be leaders in society. Their value systems and attitudes should be used as examples of how *not* to live one's life.

WRAPPING UP

While we are all waiting for this to happen young executives aspiring to senior management posts should sit back and decide how many sacrifices they are prepared to make in their lives in order to 'get on'. They should seek to work for companies which have a more complete view of life and where business success is combined with a concept of life success.

Stand up now for your children and for your life. Do not let the pathetic standards of past generations of business leaders take you and your family down the road that they have travelled. Our children need us to break the cycle of deceit so that they can grow up in an environment where time with children and the family are treated as the most important 'thing' in people's lives.

6

Father-friendly companies

During the 1980s the term 'family friendly' came into vogue. It was initially used to describe organisations which had adopted certain practices and policies which were beneficial to the family, such as maternity and birth leave, on-site childcare, flexible work hours, job-sharing work options and counselling.

SOME GAINS FOR THE FAMILY

Not all companies adopted such policies, even though research had proved that such policies could help the organisation as well as the employee. Lower levels of absenteeism and voluntary resignations were found to occur in organisations that had adopted family-friendly policies. Lowering voluntary resignations alone ensured that employee-training expenses were lower and thus the employer saw a financial gain attributable to their implementation of these policies.

Of course, morale was also found to be much higher in companies that had begun to address the fact that their employees had families and these families had needs. In a national study of fifty-eight employers in the U.S., thirty-one claimed that family-friendly policies helped attract desirable employees. Three-quarters claimed such policies lowered absenteeism. Two-thirds felt they improved worker attitudes. As Arlie Hochschild observed in *The Time Bind*:

All in all there is mounting evidence that family friendly policies add value to a company in terms of higher levels of productivity and lower levels of sickness and voluntary resignations.

Some policies supporting the family were written into law, thus ensuring organisations were forced to accord at least some recognition to the special needs of families. The sharp end of the legislation was focused on maternity leave and the career track of mothers who left to have a baby and wanted to return. Organisations which had only in the last thirty years begun to accept the legitimate concept of careers for women were now motivated to consider the needs of women who wanted to have children and maintain a career.

Following the introduction of more reasonable approaches to the issue of maternity leave, the discussion moved to the issue of childcare. On-site childcare centres became part of the employee benefits package offered by large corporations (initially in the U.S.) where the staff numbers could justify the costs of such a centre. Over time the issue became one of support for childcare as opposed to necessarily building a childcare centre, thus ensuring all employees were considered and not those who happened to work at large sites. While childcare support and extended maternity leave did start to address the needs of the working mother two issues arose.

GOING DOWN THE MUMMY TRACK

The first was that of the 'mummy track'. Women who had made use of family-friendly policies, especially flexible work hours, found themselves on a different career path. They were no longer considered to be major players, having 'given up' and allowed the family (i.e. child) to take at least some priority in their lives.

Much has been written about the 'mummy track'. There is no question that some companies treat women employees (in particular executive women employees) differently once they have decided to modify their work to incorporate the new baby. Women who continue to perform their work duties in the same way post-child as they did pre-child suffer less from the stigma of being on the 'mummy track' but still hit the well-known Australian business phenomenon, the glass ceiling.

We have a long way to go in terms of how we manage our businesses before executives are promoted because of their efforts in terms of business, family and community areas, and not their sex. The fact that someone who looks for ways to still be a committed employee as well as a committed mother is then sidelined shows how shallow our business culture is.

SUPPORT FROM THE LAW AND ON THE JOB

The second issue is the continuing need for greater legislative and workplace support. Companies which operate in industries where talented employees are scarce will be forced to adopt a much more family-friendly approach because their employees are demanding such policies. Specifically, in industries where women are increasingly taking a more significant number of key roles their employers will have to modify their behaviour or lose valuable employees. It's unfortunate that the reason for taking positive action appears to be the fear of losing good employees rather than a desire to help ensure families are more adequately cared for.

In industries where a ready supply of employees is always available, legislative support for family-friendly policies is required. We can't assume that employers will incur greater short-term costs associated with such policies on the basis of some expected future benefit.

Where they can easily recruit and train new employees examples have shown that employers take the easy option of forcing a work regime on their employees as opposed to developing a new family friendly work ethic. Why? Because the employees are more concerned about losing their job and so will toe the line.

STILL A LONG WAY TO GO

Policies which support the family are still at the formative stage in Australia. We have developed an understanding that maternity leave is a fair thing, but when it comes to issues such as paternity leave and childcare support, the private sector, on the whole, says they are matters for government.

The private sector's general lack of concern about these questions tells us a lot about the style and substance of our leading business executives. Hopefully this is a passing phase and as the current crop of leaders move on we will see a more enlightened approach.

There can be little doubt that eventually companies in Australia will see the provision of childcare support as a basic employee benefit and not some 'extra' that they should resist granting come what may. Moreover, they will not only see the benefits to themselves in terms of reduced employee direct costs (absenteeism etc) but realise they will be also contributing to the welfare of the next generation of Australians. It's interesting that some companies will fall over themselves to sponsor major sporting events under the auspices of 'helping young Australians' and yet they baulk at providing something more tangible and real—childcare support for all.

SHORT-TERM COSTS—LONG-TERM BENEFITS

One of the problems with family-friendly policies is that they only provide benefits to the organisation over the medium to long term. Over the short term all they do is increase costs and force an uncomfortable change in culture on the management of the company.

In an organisation or industry that is very focused on short-term profit there will never be any level of support for policies which assist the family. It is too easy to reject everything that hasn't been stipulated by law and to force employees to adopt a work ethic which does not acknowl-edge the family's needs. It is also too easy to use the excuse of 'tighter economic conditions' to rid the company of pro-grams that suggest in any way working fewer hours or working in a more flexible way.

As with most issues which require a fundamental change of approach, any change will require the chief executive to be personally committed to the concept of policies that support the family. This will only occur in Australia if there is a consensus amongst the CEOs of our leading companies that a real shift in attitude is required. While there are some isolated signs of movement in this respect in Australia, our current group of business leaders is unlikely to bring about overall change.

Thus the adoption of family-friendly policies across Australia is not in any way guaranteed. The combination of a government intent on letting the private sector deter-mine its own position, short-term business goals and busi-ness leaders who are not true believers when it comes to the need for family support policies does not augur well for the battle ahead.

BUT FATHER TRAILS THE FIELD

Despite the positive gains that have been made, little has been done by our leaders (mostly men) to help fathers better balance work and family needs. The majority of changes brought about in the Australian workplace assists the mother or assists the father to assist the mother. There are virtually no policies adopted in corporate Australia where the father's needs have been addressed.

Given the fact that most companies have yet to fully

accept the need for any family-friendly policies, maybe it's not surprising that father-specific policies aren't even on the radar screen. The battle for broad acceptance of policies that ensure a working mother-to-be is provided for adequately both before and after she gives birth is the first thing that needs to be tackled. Yet while this issue works its way through the parts of society that are still being Neanderthal in their approach to working women, we must also bring forward the debate on father-friendly work policies.

THE DADDY TRACK: GOING NOWHERE FAST

One problem with many family-friendly policies, is that of perception. Business management doesn't yet approve of women who take the 'mummy track', let alone men who attempt to take the 'daddy track'. The 'daddy track' actually ends up being a track that goes nowhere, ensuring that its travellers' careers are put on permanent hold.

There is a certain lack of logic in this. Businesses are still more often than not run by men. Business leaders are more often than not fathers. One would therefore expect, perhaps naively, that male business leaders would support others of their kind who wanted both to have a career and spend time with their children. Unfortunately this does not seem to be the case. Male senior managers, regardless of their own personal experiences as fathers, seem more to support the 'open all hours' attitude to executive work than to incorporate some of the very real needs of fathers.

There is much research that points to management being quite anti-father even in situations where the same company has accepted (albeit grudgingly) mother-friendly policies. The Australian academics Russell, Durkin and Savage found in a survey a significant difference in the response between managers and non-managers with respect to work-family issues. Specifically only eight per cent of male managers believed that fathers should be entitled to fifty-two weeks' unpaid leave from the birth of the child, whereas more than twice as many non-managers (eighteen per cent) agreed with this proposition. Fifty-two per cent of non-managers agreed that fathers should be entitled to five days' unpaid 'special family leave' per year to look after a sick child or meet their children's school requirements, but only thirty-two per cent of managers. Twenty-six per cent of non-managers agreed that 'providing men with paternity leave will help promote greater sharing of domestic responsibilities between men and women', as against only eleven per cent of managers. Forty per cent of non-managers felt that employers should be more responsive to their employees' problems in balancing work and family responsibilities, while only twenty-two per cent of managers agreed.

Interestingly, when women managers and non-managers were asked these questions, there was nowhere near the same degree of difference in their responses. In most cases they both recorded results very close to those of male non-managers. Even more significantly, in some cases they were more supportive of greater allowance being made for fathers in the workforce than were male non-managers. In all cases they were more sympathetic than male managers.

TILL DEATH DO US PART

My own experiences conform quite strongly to the findings of Russell, Savage and Durkin. In all but a very few cases I found the majority of the managers I worked with at the time (all of them male) basically endorsed the 'executive work ethic'. The only permissible family issues that could interrupt work were literally death or life-threatening crises. There was never any appreciation that perhaps men might want to look at similar changes in their work patterns to those which were available to women. At one company, where the management team was straight out of the 1950s macho club, there was no leeway for fathers and yet it was acceptable for mothers to take maternity leave and have time off for a sick child. Of course, this same management group did not fully accept women as senior managers, unless they acted as the men did (work obsessive hours, travel non-stop and drink heavily).

While I have observed more professional managers in recent years, there remains in Australia a culture in executive circles under which the father is expected to perform his work duties with no change in his family status. It is as though these managers really believe that the performance of any company is more important than the bond between a father and his child.

Studies in the U.S. have found that a request for unpaid leave to take care of a sick child was significantly less likely to be granted if the request came from a father rather than a mother. Even in companies which did grant all employees such leave, men were less inclined to take advantage of it than women. The general feeling was that men felt even more than women that taking leave in such circumstances could jeopardise their careers.

In Sweden, on the other hand, where there is widespread acceptance of paternity programs, the participation rate is close to fifty per cent. The huge difference between rates of participation in Sweden and places like the U.S. and Australia is the result of two factors—legislative support for paternity programs and extensive public education campaigns to promote them.

IT ALL GETS BACK TO THE WORK ETHIC

It's still not accepted as normal in our society that a father would want to spend more time with his child and less at work. The work ethic of complete dedication to the company, accompanied by long hours, is strongly entrenched as the guiding principle for men beginning their climb up the corporate ladder. There's little point in such circumstances in asking men if they want to take time off work to spend with their children. In answering the question the father has to come to terms with the value system he has been taught to accept and which is reinforced wherever he looks. Of course, at a deep level all fathers want to be with their children. But these feelings can be easily overshadowed when a man is confronted with a choice between expressing them in practice and giving up the role he has been told since birth is his main concern—work.

Before we can be certain that men would in fact spend more time with their children, if they had the opportunity, we need to create the kind of infrastructure and social values which would allow them to choose between a mix of career and family time without fear of career retribution or family retribution.

Career retribution is swift and telling and it is delivered in short order. Family retribution takes a long time. It takes many years for a child to give up trying to be with its father or to feel that it has no need for him. Thus if there is any sense that career retribution is possible, men will in general choose family retribution over career retribution. In fact, many will convince themselves that when choosing career over family they are not really dismissing their families but just delaying carrying out a promise. Such is the power that work and career have over men. Work defines their self-esteem, place in society and place in the family. Threaten this and everything else takes second place.

We have to create social structures which reinforce the role of the father and allow fathers to spend more time with their children. This will only happen when we have companies and corporations which go beyond being family-friendly (which today really means only mother-friendly) and become father-friendly as well. Once we have established organisations which do not trade off an individual's career for his family we can then allow fathers (and mothers) to determine the balance they really desire between work and family.

WHAT MAKES A FATHER-FRIENDLY COMPANY?

The concept of a father-friendly company is based on a number of assumptions about both fathers and companies. The most important of these are as follows:

- If fathers had more time with their children we would have less crime and lower levels of youth suicide.
- Children need their fathers as much as they need their mothers.
- As they are growing up boys in particular need a lot of time with their fathers.
- The relationships within a family are much stronger if the father is around instead of always being absent.
- Productivity and not work hours is what counts to a business.
- Businesses are responsible for taking into account an employee's needs with regard to his family when structuring work.
- Less than ten per cent of a working week is made up of absolutely critical, must-do-now meetings or appointments.
- Ninety per cent of day-to-day work activities should be able to be moved to accommodate family issues.
- Employees who regularly work more than fifty-five hours a week are not as valuable to a business as those who live a more balanced life.
- Companies must take responsibility for developing community values and not just achieving improved financial performance.

Let's look at some of the issues underlying these assumptions.

Companies and Community Spirit

By their articles of association and very nature companies are responsible to their shareholders. Accordingly shareholders are interested in a return on their investment. There exists no link between the ultimate owners of a business (the shareholders) and the employees. It is therefore difficult to enforce a culture of 'community spirit' or 'family understanding' on companies. They can easily point to the issue of increased costs and their responsibility to shareholders as a way around being more responsible to their employees and the community generally. Thus we are left with an almighty individual, the chief executive, who has invariably accepted this ethos.

Inherent in the introduction of any father-friendly policy is acceptance of the idea that companies should keep fathers away from their children for as little time as possible. This would ensure that companies focus more on productivity and balance leading to long-term profits than sheer work performance, as such, leading only to increased short-term profits.

Companies also need to acknowledge that families exist for twenty-four hours a day, seven days a week and not just at bonus or company picnic time. I have seen many companies which force work regimens on their staff which only turn the families of those staff against the employer. The employer then hosts a yearly picnic and expects this gesture (complete with jumping castle and free ice creams) to make up for the large number of lost weekends and long trips throughout the prior year. Family life is not broken up into events that occur

> **with business-like precision. It is made up of the day-to-day interaction between spouses and their children.**

THE TYRANNY OF MEETINGS

Accepting that a father may want to participate in the morning or evening ritual which goes on in all families would require a change in the way meetings are scheduled in a company. Being part of the morning or evening ritual should not be discounted as unimportant. I have found that some of the most important discussions with my children have occurred over toast in the morning, in the car taking them to school or at night over dinner. Children seem to need to have time and space before they open up with their issues. Being part of the normal morning landscape allows the father to be there when a child wants to talk about something that is on its mind. If you are not part of the regular environment then you miss out on key communication opportunities with your children.

Regular morning meetings should not start until after 9 a.m. Scheduling meetings regularly for 8 a.m., or even before, sends the message that if you are a father you have no chance of being involved in your child's morning ritual. If a father has to drop a child off at childcare then he will need time to get it settled and then head off to work. It is very unfortunate that company work practices have formed the basis upon which early morning childcare is now provided. Delivering a child to a centre at any time before 8 a.m. forces a regime on young children which does not allow them a normal period to wake up and get ready for the day. It forces children to become part of the ridiculous schedule adults have let themselves be trapped into. Ensuring that meetings were not scheduled until after 9 a.m. would indicate to employees that management understood some fathers (and mothers) wanted to drop their children off at childcare at a reasonable time of the day.

When I have raised this idea with some company leaders, more often than not the response is that it is essential that such meetings start very early, to set the agenda for the day. Except in exceptional circumstances (e.g. briefings before a market opens), this is a simplistic approach to time management and does not in any way utilise modern communications to solve the problem. Having a status meeting at 10 a.m. is no different in terms of production and performance than having it at 8 a.m. If the response is that meetings need to be held outside time dealing directly with customers then one has to question the amount of such time expected of the employee and whether the requirements on the employee are in fact reasonable. It also brings into question the need for the meeting in the first place. Efficient use of personal computers on networks allows for information dissemination and communication where people can manage their schedules according to real priorities and not arcane meeting rules.

Equally, holding regular meetings that go after 5:30 p.m. sends the message that any parent who wants to be a 'player' will need to sacrifice his or her evening time with children. Ensuring that such meetings were completed prior to 5:30 p.m. would allow parents to be home in time to participate to some degree in the evening ritual with children. Companies which enforce both early morning and late afternoon meetings are clearly anti-family and show a complete lack of understanding for the role of parents.

If a company must maintain either early morning or late afternoon meetings because of industry reasons (e.g. stock-brokers' briefing sessions before the market opens), then they should ensure the corresponding time in the other part of the day is left free of formal meetings. Companies must send a message to employees that says they think it's important for parents to spend time at either breakfast or dinner with their family.

EXPECTED WORKING HOURS

It's not uncommon to hear of executives working sixty to seventy or even eighty hours a week. Why does there seem to be a general acceptance that such work hours are normal practice? The answer lies less in the fact that the job requires such hours and more in the executives' inability to manage their time more effectively.

When I have challenged the work regime of some colleagues the response is generally that 'the job requires this level of commitment'. It does seem strange that all executive roles seem to require a minimum commitment of sixty or seventy hours. Why not ninety or even 100 hours a week? Or at the other end of the scale, why don't some need forty hours a week? I suspect that at seventy hours the people concerned are giving all of their energy and commitment to the job and have no more left. It has nothing to do with the job itself demanding seventy hours.

Having spent many years observing some of Australia's leading business executives manage their time, I believe there is no question that any executive role in Australia could in fact be done in forty to fifty hours a week. Any commitment beyond this is purely at the discretion of the executive and the only reason it is not challenged is the general approach of management that more work hours (as long as payment is not on an hourly basis) are a good thing. If Harry can work for eighty hours a week then great!

Management has a responsibility to break the work-hour commitment matrix that exists today. We have to start by understanding that employees are most productive only when they have a supportive family behind them and a wider perspective than merely that of the work environment. As managers we have a responsibility to help develop employees not only to utilise their skills but also to carry out their responsibilities as fathers, spouses, friends and community members.

Despite having worked in the fast-paced industry of information technology, I still believe that any job can be done effectively within a commitment of forty to fifty hours per week. It is all about how you allocate time and how you measure success. Measuring performance on reasonably expected output rather than on hours worked is central to moving away from an hours-based work culture.

Whenever I have taken over a group to manage I always make the same statement:

'If someone feels they have to work more than forty or fifty hours a week on a regular basis then we need to work together to see what is going wrong. From time to time extra effort will be required but you have my commitment that these periods will be rare and of a limited length. I want people to work here, be productive, have fun and then get out of here and enjoy their real life with family and friends. My priorities are my family, my health and then my job. This does not mean I am not committed to my work, it just means that I understand what the important things in life are.'

PATERNITY LEAVE

Fathers should be offered paternity leave of at least six weeks on full pay at any time during the first year of the baby's life. Paternity leave must be on full pay. Providing such leave at less than full pay provides families with an economic imperative not to take paternity leave. The father's normal income must be maintained during the period of leave. I can already hear the wails of protest from the economic rationalists in Australia. Inherent in such a scheme is the idea that we need to value a parent's time with his or her new baby. We have partially addressed this issue for mothers but we have done nothing for fathers.

Paternity leave provides benefits to the father, the child and society generally. In Sweden it is felt that their parental-leave policy, which incorporates paternity leave, is the single most important factor in increasing fathers' participation in family life. When a father spends his parental leave with his child—for a period of at least three months—he invariably develops an independent relationship with the child and remains closely involved with it when he returns to work.

Unfortunately the mere provision of paternity leave itself does not solve the problem. Less than five per cent of fathers who are eligible for paternity leave in the U.S. and U.K. actually take it. The Swedish participation rate of around fifty per cent is the result of an education program to persuade the community generally that it was a good thing. Education will help motivate fathers to take the time to which they are entitled, but it could have the result of convincing fathers in the public sector while having no effect on those in the private sector.

It is tempting to force fathers to take such leave whether they want to or not, in order to make sure everyone participates rather than only a few who would then run the risk of finding themselves on the 'daddy track'. This will not work. The only way to succeed is to lead from the top. Senior managers must establish a culture where it is expected that a new father will take the time off to be with his baby. Those who do not should be counselled for choosing to ignore their babies and not in any way praised for some misguided sense of loyalty to the company.

PART-TIME WORK

Increasingly in two-income families both parents will want to spend more time with their children. It is becoming a more accepted practice for women to return to part-time work at some point following the birth of their children, yet we have a very long way to go. Employers have to think more positively about drawing on the resources of the large number of women who left the workforce to have children and now can't find a suitable part-time job.

For men we are at ground zero. There are few part-time roles that men can hope for if they want to reduce their work-time to spend more time with their families. The choice for professional and management-level men is to stop work totally or keep working full-time. Perhaps if a significant proportion of men were able to convert their roles to part-time work, this would also create more part-time opportunities for women to fill, to the obvious benefit of both sexes. It would also allow husbands and wives to plan their careers around the time commitment they want to make to their children at various stages of the latter's lives. Such flexibility for both parents ensures that they can participate equally in their children's development while continuing with their own careers.

FAMILY LEAVE

Once you have a family your responsibilities increase significantly. Parents of young children will naturally have more demands on their time than will adults without children. Separable from the demands of taking care of their own parents, the demands of work and the normal household duties the working parent will have at least some of the following demands on their time: attendance at school events (concerts, education week, sporting carnivals); involvement in school day activities (canteen, reading programs); attending to a sick child; and being available for meetings with teachers.

The normal work schedule assumes that people are available five days a week, forty-eight weeks a year from 9 a.m. to 5 p.m. In companies with management that is more understanding of the demands of being a parent a more flexible approach to time management is allowed. Yet there exist even more companies where it is not considered acceptable for an employee (especially a male) to take time off for a child-related activity. We need to first accept that fathers do want to attend important events in their child's life and that this will require a level of understanding on behalf of the employer. As with paternity leave employers need to allocate formal time that can be taken off by employees with children so that the parent can attend the child's events. The regime should not allow parents to use this time to do things other than attend the child-related activities.

THE ROLE OF SENIOR MANAGEMENT

For an organisation to become more family-friendly and then more father-friendly it will require a significant change in its culture. Senior management in companies need to believe in the principle that as a society we need to work out ways for fathers to be able to spend more time with their children. Unless company management takes on board this idea seriously, no amount of government legislation will help change anything. Given the increasingly significant role that work is playing in men's lives, it is the work environment that has to change to accommodate the needs of fathers and their children. A company does not change primarily in response to community attitudes but because management changes the structures that support its culture, including its value and reward systems and the way it approaches its employees.

Thus the role of the management of a company, and specifically its chief executive, is crucial in any change towards a more father-friendly organisation. We know that if we can modify the attitude of the top management of a company, then we will achieve wholesale change within the company. We move from having to worry about convincing large numbers of people of the benefits of family-friendly approaches to only having to influence a comparative handful. Unfortunately the people we need to influence couldn't be less open to change.

In most cases the senior executives of companies are older men who have long since established a pattern for their own family relationships. Research in the U.S. found that senior, older, male executives were less supportive of issues such as work-family balance than were younger executives. The older executives had brought up their children under a particular regime of communication and involvement and believed that since both they and their children survived the process there was no basis for modifying company attitudes towards a more balanced approach to work. The same was found in relation to support for assistance in home duties. More often than not the executive had a stay-at-home wife as well as a personal secretary. Between the two of them, these women were able to ensure the executive never had to deal with real-life issues and domestic duties. The eventual result was a senior executive who lived a life quite divorced from the reality of most of the population. Again younger executives who had stay-at-home wives were obviously more confronted by the question of balancing domestic duties and were, not surprisingly, more supportive of changes in company policies to cater to work-family issues.

ENDING THE GENERATION GAP

These older senior executives hold the keys to their organisations' culture and reward system. They exercise enormous influence over what is accepted practice in an organisation. They are also people who have dedicated their lives to their companies, having in many cases sacrificed marital relationships, time with their children and personal hobbies for the material rewards of corporate life. It would be wonderful to think that they could look back objectively on their lives and see the mistakes they have made with regard to priorities. From time to time we do see examples of such wisdom, men who have spoken publicly about how they put work before everything else during their career and how wrong this was. But there are very few others of his kind who seem able to see that they have been operating under an incorrect value system. The great majority seem to believe that the way they conducted their lives worked for them and this gave them the right to 'force' it on their employees.

Steve Biddulph believes that it will take five generations to significantly change attitudes in Australian business culture with regard to the father's role in society. It is depressing to think that we have to wait for the present crop of senior executives to die off before they can be replaced by younger men whose values have been affected more by their desire to be good fathers than to be powerful and make money. However, there is also a chance that the prevailing culture of companies will not die out with their present management teams, but will live on driven by the recruiting and reward systems they have established.

THE POWER OF THE MAGIC MOMENT

Perhaps I'm naive, but I believe that if you can persuade men to start to spend more time with their children and you can get them to look back honestly on their years as fathers, we may see change earlier and more profoundly across business Australia. All that is needed is for them to experience a magic moment.

This moment could be full of joy or full of sadness. The effect is the same. It could be the first time they are in the school playground alone with a bunch of kids and after some trepidation they let go and start to have fun. It could be the first time they take their child to pre-school and they see the child bursting with pride because its dad has come to school. It could be the first time they realise how little time and energy they have given their children so far and resolve to mend their ways. It could be the first time they look back on their childhood and realise that they really did want to spend more time with their own fathers, and begin to regret that they did not get the opportunity.

Such moments would have a more powerful effect on changing the attitude of senior executives than will any set of seminars, books like this or government legislation. They would then flow on to help create new value systems, without which any permanent shift in company thinking is impossible. Without a change in the value system companies that move towards more father-friendly structures will, at the first sign of economic downturn, come scurrying back to the old ways.

HIGHER COSTS, BUT GREATER BENEFITS

There is no doubt that introducing paternity leave, family leave, part-time work and similar policies will add to companies' costs, at least marginally. In an age of shrinking margins any idea that increases a cost base tends to be cast aside fairly quickly. Such policies are only accepted if management believes that they are no longer just 'nice to have' but are 'must dos'. Then they become part of the fixed, accepted cost structure. Time is then spent on other parts of the organisation's costs areas to look for savings that can ensure profit retention.

It could also be argued that in adopting these 'must do' policies companies will over time see much lower rates of voluntary resignation and higher productivity due to the greater loyalty of appreciative employees. That may seem a cynical view, but for whatever reason at some point in time society has to step back from the rush to economic rationalism as the sole precept on which businesses and nations are run.

CREATING FATHER FRIENDLY COMPANIES

Chief executives who want to make their companies more father-friendly will find that they are in fact making the company more family-friendly. The required actions are often more about modifying the culture than about new expensive human resource policies (although there are some of those also!). Here are a few ideas:

- Do not call regular meetings that start before 9 a.m. or after 4 p.m. By doing this the company is actively acknowledging that some fathers may want to drop their kids at school or be home to have dinner with their children.
- Do not expect employees to travel more than five weeks a year (ie thirty-five nights in total). Even this is high and at this rate the father's relationship with their family will suffer. Thirty-five nights away a year should be the extreme.
- Allow employees who travel to have make up days.

Allow them one day off for every three away.

- Give employees half a day off per school term to attend their child's school. Not for the events but just to hang out and help with canteen, reading, etc.
- Provide generous paternity leave for new fathers.
- Have an annual father-child day at the workplace where fathers are encouraged to bring their kids to work so they see what their father does during the day. (Of course we should have the same for working mothers.)
- Motivate employees to take their annual holidays. People who do not take them should be counselled, not applauded.
- Establish a culture where weekend work is discouraged except in truly emergency situations.
- Create an environment where employees are very, very rarely interrupted while they are on holidays. Such interruptions should be frowned upon.
- Talk about families a lot during company meetings and presentations. Create the real understanding that people have families first and jobs second.

WRAPPING UP

We are not employees first and last. We are members of a society first and last, who work both to keep ourselves alive and to express ourselves creatively in some way. The development of the industrial society over the last 100 years or so has seen a continual erosion of the role of the father and an increased emphasis placed on the importance of one's job. We have a choice on how we approach the next 100 years. We can continue as we are and watch our children grow up in fatherless environments, our companies become even harsher in their pursuit of profit and our society succumb to pressures and problems we have never experienced before.

The acceptance of the role of the father and the modification of the work environment to allow fathers to play a more involved role in their children's lives can help to reverse the negative trends that exist today. Companies and their senior management are the key to the way we will move forward. Specifically, chief executives of organisations have in their power the ability to make our society a better place for children and their fathers and mothers, if only their actions moving forward were driven as much by a sense of their human and social responsibilities as their business acumen.

7

What makes a good father?

I t is hard to imagine that any fathers down through time have not wanted to be known as 'good' fathers, either from a desire for public recognition or some deeper motivation based on feelings of love and devotion.

There are very few books that really help you determine what you need to do if you want to be a good father. There are lots of books that deal with parenting, but they seem to be more concerned with mothering than fathering. I am told the reason for this is that men do not look for books about parenting and even less for books on what it takes to be a good father. Books such as *Manhood* by Steve Biddulph, which discusses men's role in life, are more often bought by women, read and then passed to their husbands, sons or fathers. Even *Manhood* does not clearly deal with the role of fatherhood in a way which helps the novice father work out what he should be trying to do.

It would be silly to pretend that all fathers are good fathers, particularly when fathering is so difficult to evaluate. Nonetheless, I know people who will go out of their way to defend any sort of behaviour. 'Sure, Bill comes home drunk some nights and screams at his kids and, okay, he also spends more time fishing than he does with his kids, but when he is at home and sober he's a great dad', some of them will even say.

This may be an extreme example, but fathering is not a part-time activity which can be broken up into compartments to accommodate the sporting, work or leisure pursuits of men. Nor is it a responsibility that can accept such aberrations as physical and emotional abuse, alcoholic rages or significant periods away from the children. Good fathering is a commitment which goes for twenty-four hours a day, seven days a week and fifty-two weeks a year. But what exactly does it comprise?

GOOD DADS AND NOT-SO-GOOD DADS

In trying to differentiate good fathering from bad fathering with so little expert advice available, definition is easiest at the extreme ends of the spectrum. A father who systematically abuses his children physically and emotionally is clearly a bad father. Equally one who puts his children's physical and emotional welfare above material or career goals would obviously be seen as a good father. Yet while the 'bad' end of the scale is easy to quantify, it is harder to be specific about the 'good' end. An alcoholic child basher is easy to identify, but where is the model of the 'good' father?

What about a father who works normal hours and then spends most nights and weekends working in a voluntary capacity with the S.E.S. or the local sports club where his children play? This father is not work-obsessed, he allocates time to community activities that involve his children and yet he spends very little time with them away from the sports club. Where does such a father fit into the spectrum?

Years ago when our eldest daughter went to pre-school, I noted two examples of this type of parental behaviour. One mother had four children born quite close together and yet she was on the pre-school social committee and executive committee, as well as various committees at the school her oldest child attended. She would spend long nights making items for the pre-school fête and then manage stalls all day to help sell items. She saw herself as being a fabulous mother who was significantly helping her children's school community. Yet she spent little time with her kids and would often scream at them when they 'bothered' her while she was serving at a stall or doing some other duty.

A father at the pre-school was similarly heavily involved in all manner of activities and, because of his very heavy work schedule, it meant that most of his time with his kids was spent there. The difference between these two parents was that the father would always want to have his children with him and the mother seemed to see hers as a distraction from her duties. Yet both parents gave of themselves to the school.

How should we classify such parents who give up so much of their time and energy to help community projects? They are clearly very public-spirited and without their efforts many facilities around our neighbourhoods would not exist. As regards these two people, probably no-one would disagree that they were good parents in relation to carrying out their school responsibilities, but it would be hard to say the same about the mother concerning her attitude to her children.

What about the father who is very successful at business and makes sure his children have the best of everything, whether that is measured by the schools they attend, the clothes they wear, the make of bikes they ride and so on? Other people who put more store on providing children with material possessions than I do might rate him highly, but my evaluation of him would be different.

All these examples apply in varying respects to the great majority of parents, who exhibit both good and bad qualities in their parenting to some degree or other. Very few parents are really bad parents, like the small number of people who abuse their children physically and emotionally and who do not deserve to be blessed with the gift of children. The rest of us are somewhere in the middle, trying to be good parents but sometimes not succeeding.

THE FALLACY OF THE GOOD PROVIDER

'A good father is one who provides financial security for his family,' commented one senior executive to whom I put the question. 'That's it. With financial security the family can live in a safe neighbourhood, the children can attend the best schools and meet the right people who will be important as they grow up.'

In a society which is becoming increasingly money-motivated and economically rational the importance of financial security in the overall wellbeing of children needs to be examined. While the provision of money does ensure the family will never starve, it seems somewhat simplistic to make it the major determinant of good fathering. I know of many fathers in senior positions who bring home mounds of cash and yet their families are lacking in many ways. As we have seen, the provider model is also a great escape mechanism for fathers who are not able to regulate their work environment properly. They can always point to the fruits of their labour and the benefit such wealth brings the family. Anyway, many argue, money is so much more measurable than stability, self-esteem, emotional security, love, understanding or such intangible factors.

The idea of the good father being a good provider does have validity for certain sections of society. Families which are really struggling to survive do not have the opportunity to rearrange their work schedules to accommodate their children. For them the money coming in often does not even meet their basic needs. Their main concern is surviving in an environment where employment security has disappeared. Money is managed on a daily basis and allocated to mere essentials.

But this is certainly not the case for the thousands of fathers in middle to senior management posts in Australia. Where a family has been able to move from struggling for survival to a lifestyle which incorporates having the 'good things in life', clearly the money required to provide for a basic living is far less than that brought home. Fathers in the fortunate position of holding well-paid executive jobs are involved in purchasing decisions over goods and services far removed from the basic necessities of life.

Executives who have achieved financial success have a choice. They have chosen to continue to work increasingly longer hours to provide more money for themselves and their families. They have chosen to establish a more expensive lifestyle and then need to be able to fund this lifestyle. But they have not looked at their lives in toto and worked out whether their commitment to work is hurting their family relationships.

Sadly, as many executives tell me, they see themselves still as providers, needing to work as long and as hard as ever for their family. They are unfortunately both confused and misled. They are confused because they have lost their perspective of what makes up a basic life and how much money is required to maintain this life. They are misled because they have allowed themselves to be persuaded that they really need a bigger house or a better car regardless of the effect the continued effort to provide them will have on their families.

They have been misled into believing that their family really needs these extensions to a basic life. Yet their families did not get a chance to vote on this. Their son, who is still young enough to yearn for his father's attention, does not get a vote. His daughter, who desperately wants to have a strong bond with her father, doesn't get a vote; and neither does the dutiful wife who has supported her husband through the early part of his career.

SEEING LIFE WITH NEW EYES

One of the keys to becoming a good father is to pull yourself out of your daily grind and attempt to see your life with some form of perspective. Easy to say, hard to do. A wake-up call in the form of a major tragedy will often shake people out of the momentum of their daily lives. Yet it would be awful to believe that the only way to get men to step back and look more clearly at their lives was to wait for a life-changing event to occur.

- *Give yourself time to reflect.* Taking even brief periods out of the day gives you the opportunity to think about your life and where it is going. In particular, just sit down and contemplate things for a while and ask yourself these questions. Are you happy? Are you communicating your feelings to your wife? Do you like your job? What can you do to make it more enjoyable? How much time have you spent with the kids in the last couple of weeks? How many times have you had long chats with them in recent weeks? Do you know what issues they are dealing with and what problems they are trying to solve? Are you being the sort of parent that you had wanted to be?
- *Get to know the lives of the people around you.* Often I have found that learning about the lives of my colleagues has helped me think more deeply about my own life. The façade erected in the work environment can lead you to believe that everyone is leading a stable life with no traumas. Learning that a workmate has a sick wife or child who requires constant attention or understanding the difficulties a new colleague's family are having following their move from interstate really helps you put your own problems into proper perspective.

Seeing colleagues interact with their families also helps you understand issues in your own relationships. At times I have become friendly with a work colleague and have then watched him with his family. Sometimes I am quite concerned at how some executives treat their wives and children. In the work environment you may know Joe

Shmuck as a focused, bright executive who deals well with staff and delivers results on time. But at home, Joe is dismissive of his wife, inattentive to his children's needs and only uses home as a rest stop between work shifts. By being able to see Joe both at home and at work you get a picture of a man who is work-obsessed and whose values you would not like anyone to emulate.

- *Ask your children to play the role of their dad in a game of make-believe.* If you want to understand how your children see you, then this is the way. It only takes one game with 'Daddy' not actually being in it (because he's at work all the time), snoring his head off in a lounge chair or reading the paper while the rest of the family is busy doing things, or screaming at the 'kids' for no reason whatsoever to realise that perhaps you are not quite the attentive father you thought you were.

It's hard to imagine anything more fulfilling than a morning spent with a young child playing make-believe in the backyard, having a surf together, going on a walk with the dogs or just sitting and talking about life. It's like a tonic to have been admitted even for a brief time to the world of children. You can't live there forever, nor should you, but you can use these times to continually be reminded of the beauty of children and why we, as adults, have a responsibility to leave the world a better place for them.

GIVE THEM *REAL* TIME, NOT PHONEY TIME

Surely if given the choice of spending an extra three hours in some intergalactic business meeting or spending three hours playing with their children all fathers would choose the latter. Yet this choice is being made every day in offices across Australia and invariably the first option is taken. The business meeting takes precedence in all but 'event' situations.

Yet randomly deciding to give up work completely to spend all your time with your children is not the right answer. Nor will it necessarily make you a good father. Nobody can say categorically how much time with children is the 'right' time. I know that when our first daughter was born I wanted someone to tell me exactly how much time I should spend with her. Fifteen years on I have learned that the right amount of time depends on the situation and how the time is spent.

The father who leaves home early, gets back late, travels constantly and works part of the weekend is not spending the right amount of time with his children. Any father who maintains such a schedule is not being responsible to his children. He has made the wrong choice between time allocated to work and time allocated to the family. Moreover, he is using his time at home purely to recuperate after a hectic and demanding working day. You can't blame him for needing to do this, but you can question his priorities.

That represents one extreme. At the other is a father who doesn't have a permanent job and thus is available for the children all the time. This may also mean he's a house-husband and does all the housework while his wife brings home the money. But the fact that a father may have more time to spend with his children does not automatically mean that he is a better father. He's obviously better than the workaholic described above, but we would have to know exactly how he makes use of that time before nominating him for the 'father of the year' award just yet.

While the idea of 'quality' time is really an excuse used by parents for their failure to look after their children properly, it's also true that just because a father is 'at home' it doesn't mean he's more involved with his children.

ACCEPTING YOUR RESPONSIBILITIES

To be able to pull back out of the daily grind and think about the direction of your life and your relationships with your family is a powerful skill which helps you to understand more of what a balanced life is all about, as well as what your children need from you at different stages in their lives. In addition to this rational thought, however, what is now required is some heartfelt emotion.

The birth of a child is a magnificent gift. Unencumbered by any of the prejudices that adults develop over their life, the newborn child has yet to be told of the limits of their abilities or how to judge other people. The child is also some link between where the parent has come from and where the child will eventually go in their life. From that first moment the parents have a wonderful opportunity to learn again about the wonderment of childhood and at the same time pass on to the child the lessons they themselves have learnt in the course of their lives. The German-American writer Alice Miller, author of *The Drama of the Gifted Child*, has summed up this link as follows:

... someday we will regard our children not as creatures to manipulate or to change but rather as messengers from a world we once deeply knew, but which we have long since forgotten, who can reveal to us more about the true secrets of life, and also our own lives, than our parents were ever able to.

After passing no exam, having paid no tuition fee or having had to sit through no searching reviews by our peers, we are given this most precious opportunity to link the past with the future and to help the world be a better place. Through having a child develop under our wing we engage in a two-way relationship which gives as much back to the parent as the parent receives from the child. For the rest of their lives the parents will be able to enjoy this wonderful relationship with someone who will carry forward something of themselves.

The process of being around children while they grow up also helps parents learn more about life. Many times friends have told me how their general attitudes have changed when they had children. In a perfect world having children would not serve as such a catalyst, but the fact remains that most people develop stronger views on many issues once they have had children.

One's immediate feelings of responsibility when a child is born can be overpowering and even quite frightening in their own way. When our first daughter arrived I recall quite vividly the emotions I felt moments after she was born. I had this baby who was only minutes old and whom I did not know in any way whatsoever. Yet I immediately felt this incredible sense of responsibility. I wanted to protect her from the bad things in life, I wanted to help her have a full and happy life. Even then my desire to nurture and protect was very strong.

Whether or not a father is touched as deeply as I was by the birth of his child, he must face up to his reponsibilities. Fathering is a life-long task that can't be cast aside in the interests of enhanced career prospects or for other mundane considerations. It is a task that requires a constant commitment of time, energy and love. It is not a task that can be dealt with tomorrow, next week, after the next budget review or when things eventually take a turn for the better. Too often I hear fathers talk about wanting to spend time with their children but saying they will do so when they can get over the busy period at work. The problem is the busy period never seems to cease to exist.

For a father to do the best for his children, he has to accept the responsibilities of fatherhood unreservedly. Unless he recognises how important the role is, he'll end up letting other parts of his life take over without realising it.

PUTTING YOUR LOVE WHERE YOUR CHILD IS

Being a father means primarily that you put your child's welfare and needs ahead of your own. This does not mean you spoil the child with gifts. On the contrary, the inattentive parent acting out of guilt often tries, as mentioned earlier, to use the latest toy or game as a means of squaring off for broken promises and absent time. Putting your child's welfare and needs ahead of your own does mean that you make it an utterly wholehearted commitment. You live a fulfilling life and have a tremendous career, but every day you think about whether you are doing as much as you should for your wife and children. Unfortunately, too often business obligations take precedence over a child's need for daily contact with its parents. If a father allows this to continue for long periods of time, he is clearly putting his own interests ahead of his family's and ignoring the responsibilities of fatherhood.

To men like my stockbroker friend who profess to love their children, but never actually see them, I always say: 'Walk the talk.' Proclamations of love and devotion without an underlying acceptance of the responsibility to develop the relationship remind me of youthful 'love affairs'—lots of emotion, much passion but little commitment beyond next Saturday night. To claim to love your child and yet choose to live a life with no sign that you really accept the responsibilities of fatherhood denotes an emotional shallowness no mature man should ever be proud of.

The Cries that Come in the Night

As a child develops there are many magical moments, beginning with its first smile as a newborn baby. While all these little incidents were important to me, some of the magic moments I can remember required lots of time and effort on my behalf.

I became quite proud of the fact that when any of our children would wake up frightened in the middle of the night, there was an equal chance that they would call out for my wife or me. This did not just happen overnight. It was the product of my spending time with them individually developing a relationship of trust where they felt comfortable with me in all situations. It was also a process that was different for each of them. With our first daughter we were settled in our home and there was nothing to distract my wife and me from spending time with her. With the second daughter things were somewhat different. We moved back to Australia when she was six weeks old and the first few months of her life were a period of constant turmoil until we settled down again.

When she was about nine months old, I began to notice that she would always prefer to be with her mother than me. I quickly realised that in our rush to re-establish a life back in Australia I had neglected to nurture a relationship with her. From that point on I devoted more time and energy on developing a feeling of love and trust between us. When she was about eighteen months old she started to call out for me about as often as she called out for my wife. In her own subtle way she was beginning to feel close to me.

This was not something I had to force myself to do, yet I was surprised to learn over time that many fathers did not try to build this kind of relationship with their children. Other fathers I knew would talk about how their children always called out for their mothers in the night and always went to their mothers if they were hurt in any way. They were obviously relieved that they could sleep through the night-time traumas. Not everyone would agree with this position, but it's only recently begun to be questioned. I used to comment that they may want to think about the fact that they were missing an opportunity to create a bond with their children that would be of immense importance to both of them.

FORGOTTEN CHILD, REJECTED DAD

I also know of situations where a child while young does not want to spend time just with its father. Invariably this is because the father has never really endeavoured to develop a relationship with the child. How often does one see a man attempting to discipline a child, obviously without any idea of how to control its behaviour. This alienation then becomes a self-fulfilling prophecy, accentuated in situations where there is no mother around. The father feels both powerless and humiliated by the experience and avoids going out in public alone with his child.

When I witness such scenes I always feel very sorry for both the father and the child. The father loves the child but does not know how to handle the situation because there is no real bond between them. The child does not feel comfortable with the father and so acts up.

OPENING YOUR HEART

Children are very perceptive creatures. Spending time with them does not by itself develop a relationship. My experience is that you need to be very open and honest with them. You need to open your heart to them in a way that they know you are being genuine about wanting to spend time with them. Again this is a difficult process. You have to expose your emotions in a way that does put you at risk of being either hurt or seen as strange.

As mentioned earlier, early in our eldest daughter's school days I would play with her and the other children in the playground. This was a risky strategy, as once you start horsing around and generally being silly the kids are liable to avoid you and you end up looking pretty stupid—and pathetic.

The key is to drop your pretensions and discard your adult posturing. I have noticed many fathers stand on the edge of the playground not sure what to do. It's clear that they want to venture out and play with the kids but something is holding them back. Some will try to join in, but they are restricted by how they think they will be viewed by others. You can sense their trepidation, and yet to really enjoy such opportunities the father has to relax and just go with the flow.

Men spend a lifetime honing their management skills and gradually master them by conscious effort and energy. The same applies to learning to relax and enjoy being with your children. Many men do not feel they have the skills to handle children properly, but they should realise they can't expect to be instant experts. With time and patience, however, the skills will come and the effort will prove to have been worthwhile.

Letting yourself go and really getting involved with children can be a daunting experience. You can't fall back on adult posturing if the kids don't react to your game or attempt to join in. Rather than being scared of a negative response, fathers should realise that if they open their hearts and minds they will be able to easily relate to their children and they will immediately feel comfortable running around a playground pretending to be a giraffe.

MY ROPE IS MY BOND

I often think of the father-child relationship as being like a rope held by two people whose strength defines the strength of the emotional bond between them. It is as though when the child is born there exists only a very fine thread with its father which could be easily snapped. But as they spend more time together more strands are added to the rope, making the bond between them stronger. Yet the rope is also one that can easily unwind if the father does not pay enough attention to making it firmer and he and his child start to drift apart as there is nothing binding them to one another.

But if, on the other hand, the father spends more and more time with his child, the rope becomes very strong and the bond between them is able to weather all the trials and tribulations of life. If the child goes off and is in danger of getting into severe trouble the rope can be pulled to bring it back to safety. Over time both parent and child thus learn to trust the rope and its strength, knowing that it is always there to be used when needed. But its durability depends on the strength it assumes in the child's early and most formative years. It is then that the father needs to devote most time to making the rope, to ensure that it will withstand the strains upon it and last forever.

HOW MUCH IS THE 'RIGHT' AMOUNT OF TIME?

Unfortunately there is no simple standard of measurement that allows us to see if we are being good enough fathers. The closest proximity to a useful measure that I have found is the time you spend with your children. This is not time spent watching a television program together but real and active time between father and child. The corollary of this is time spent at work. Not surprisingly the more time a father spends at work the less he will spend with his children.

So how much *is* the 'right' amount of time to spend with your children? It can be determined by the following framework:

- Allocate some proper time every day to spend with your children doing what they want to do. Talk about their day and what went on. Play the games they want to play. Don't do this while watching television, reading, paying bills or working on your scale model of the Eiffel Tower.
- Ensure the time is allocated when the children are most likely to be enthusiastic and energetic, not over-tired and ready for bed.
- Keep the weekends fundamentally free to spend time with the family, doing household chores as well as playing with the children. Being at home all weekend but spending every waking moment up a ladder repairing the roof or in the back shed building a model aeroplane doesn't count as family time.
- If you do have to travel take some time back. If you have been away for three or four days, then take a day off and spend the time involved in activities at your children's school or taking your child somewhere out of school on a special outing. This does not make up for being away, but it does ensure that the rope between you has time to mend and strengthen.
- Watch for signs of distress from your children. Rarely will a child be able to articulate that it feels neglected or unloved. Watch for signals from your children that they feel as though you don't care about their lives. Devote extra time to them if you see signs of distress. You will only develop this skill of knowing when your children are

out of sorts by spending lots of time with them.

- Participate in their lives. Do something regular at their school. Coach a sports team, be part of a father's canteen. Undertake the activity as much to watch and learn as to impart skills and help develop the children. Allocate these activities in your diary and place the same level of importance on such appointments as you would a board presentation.

WRAPPING UP

Good fathers are fathers who have open hearts, are acutely aware of their children's needs, make time for their children and who show their love by actions. They make terrible mistakes from time to time and they can't deliver on their promises all the time. Work will have to take precedence occasionally and they will not always be in a great mood.

However, as a result of their focused attention and expressed love their children will see them as great dads—people who make mistakes and yet people they can rely on, communicate with and love in return. When all is said and done, if children grow up with a desire to maintain a strong friendship with their fathers and want to emulate them as much as possible when they become parents, then the fathers concerned can say they did the best they could. What more can anyone hope to do?

8

Separated fathers ... separated children

C hildren without their fathers and fathers without their children. Both present challenges in their own ways. These situations could have resulted from the break-up of a marriage or relationship, or through some tragedy that saw a family lose its father. In both cases the children suffer from not having their father around and clearly where a father is separated from his children he too suffers.

But the sad fact of life is that many families do break up, through no particular fault of any party. The most common result is that the children stay with their mother and the father retains visitation rights. While from a number of perspectives the divorce or separation helps the husband-wife relationship, it also creates a new set of emotional problems. Children are affected by living in a situation where their parents' marriage has collapsed and the house is filled with tension, if not perhaps violence. Removing the cause of tension (the husband-wife relationship) ensures that the family environment can be normalised. Individually the parents are free of the source of unhappiness and the children are not subjected to unpleasant personal clashes. The price of this change in the family setting is often a lower standard of living (manageable if not desirable) and a lifelong sadness for the parent who does not have custody of the children. The father who may be left alone can choose to live his life in one of two ways. He either tries to maintain as much contact as possible through visitation rights and looking after his children every second weekend while also providing financial support for them, or he drops out of their lives altogether.

DEADBEAT DADS—OR FRUSTRATED FATHERS?

The most common stereotype of fathers separated from their children is the unfortunate term 'Deadbeat Dad'. The *National Enquirer*, a popular U.S. tabloid newspaper, makes quite a point each week of tracking down fathers who have cleared out without meeting their child-support payments. Their photos and stories of betrayal are plastered over the paper each week. And so be it. Of course, these irresponsible men should be brought to justice and they should be forced to continue to provide support for their children. Yet we do not question why they took this course of action. Were they really all bad men who fled their family responsibilities at the first available opportunity? It is clear that such an observation is not necessarily fair. Perhaps their actions are a result of their trying to cope with a very difficult situation as much as a case of their shirking responsibility.

Choosing no longer to have contact with your children is not a course of action that any person would take lightly. To suggest that such men are just trying to get out of their responsibilities is simplistic and implies that men are somehow less responsible than women. We don't realise just how heartbreaking it is for men to lose daily contact with their children. A father who wants to be deeply involved with his children cannot do so by seeing them every second weekend and for alternate weeks during school holidays. Such a process of formalised visits works to undermine the relationship between father and child. As has been pointed out earlier, children need their fathers around them every day, for extended periods of time. Anything less affects the child and, I would suggest, also the father. The energy that flows from child to parent as a result of a close relationship dries up when there is only intermittent contact.

It is not surprising to note the slow destruction of any deep relationship as the visiting process sets in. The father, initially determined to ensure the child does not suffer from being separated from him, works hard to make the visiting time 'great'. Do lots of things, buy lots of toys, go to lots of places. Yet such a plan is doomed. Of course kids want to go places and get things, but such activities are not the substance that relationships are built on. What the father needs is to be able to spend unhurried time with his children talking about what went on during their week. Children, however, do not react well to this artificial structuring of their life. They do not store up all the important moments in their week so that they can tell their father. The major events are recalled but for them life is not a set of major events strung together. It is more about the daily rituals, changes in friendships and responses to the actions of others. Even the most attentive father, when confronted by living his child's life through visiting rights, can't hope to gain as deep an understanding of it as the mother will have. Thus fathers who desire a very close relationship have to learn to cope with this far from ideal framework.

Work also plays a significant role in shaping the new form of the father-child relationship. Fathers who are newly separated from their families are more exposed to its pressures than before. Work expands to take up any time that is available and thus a life that now has a new hole where family time once resided has no trouble filling it. This introduces an unfortunate self-reinforcing pattern. Fathers work more and more of their energy and resources is diverted to work. Their interaction with their children becomes more frustrating and sadder as they are unable to make up, in one weekend, for twelve days' separation from their children. Work provides feedback which suggests even more time should be spent at it and generally the feedback loop involves the father more and more. At some point he resigns himself to the fact that he is not providing much value to his children in these tension-filled visits and starts to skip them. It is easy to condemn the father's actions as reflecting a lack of commitment, but to do so would underestimate the sadness and resignation that must drive a father not to want to spend time with his children.

Yet there must also be cases of 'Deadbeat Mums'— women who through their own irresponsible actions fail to give their children proper support. It is quite unfair only to represent separated fathers in this poor light. All it does is confirm the media-created image of separated fathers as being basically bad people.

Further confirmation is provided by the examples of fathers who in the midst of some mid-life crisis run off with a new (mostly younger) woman, leaving behind the dedicated wife and mother of their children. Again, these cases do exist and men who treat their commitments and responsibilities so lightly should be treated accordingly by society as a whole. Society, of course, fully accepts the change of partner and rarely questions the father's abdication of his responsibility to his children.

While I find this type of behaviour reprehensible I also feel quite sorry for these men. At some point they will wake up and realise how pathetic they have been and how shallow their lives have become. They will have destroyed the bond that they had with their children and while they may well have fallen out of love with their wives they will be forever haunted by the sheer lack of human decency with which they treated their former partners.

SUFFER THE LITTLE CHILDREN ...

Unfortunately the media rarely quote examples of men whose marriages have broken up and yet who remain dedicated, caring, loving fathers. Pity the husband who, while being in an unhappy marriage, deeply loves his children. In most cases, as the marriage crumbles and a settlement is agreed, the children stay with the mother and the father establishes a new lonely life. I think we underestimate the devastating sadness that comes from being separated from one's children. The children no longer have their father around and thus feel their own sense of loss.

In a situation where fathers are separated from their children, both the children and father suffer. Children need their father, or at least a father figure. Thus something must be done to help children who have lost their fathers through tragedy or whose fathers have permanently decided to not be part of their lives. It is wrong to assume that a mother can provide everything the child needs in order to develop a stable and balanced view of life. In situations where children have no father around it is important to look for father figures who can help out and be role models for children.

A good friend of mine who has three children at one point wanted to have more. When I asked him why he and his wife had decided against this, he responded: 'I realised that I can use any extra time and energy I have to provide some fatherly advice and support to kids we know who don't have a father around.' In the circle of friends that he and his wife had there were a number of mothers with children whose fathers were not around (some due to tragic accidents and some by choice). His attitude was one which should be adopted more widely. We need more men to take on 'father' roles with children other than their own.

Surrogate Fathers

Other family members, neighbours, friends, teachers and coaches can all take part in fathering children who do not have a father of their own around. It would be great to be able to assume that the man who was around when the baby was born will be there forever. For lots of reasons this is not the case. Thus we need to back fill this critical need for our children. We must not assume that the mother can fill this role or that a child can do without 'fathering'. To resign ourselves to a situation where it is considered acceptable for children to grow up without stable 'father' relationships would be tantamount to conducting a vast social experiment which would create major problems for our children and the community as a whole. Children need fatherly influence as much as they need food and water.

Mothers who have no 'father' around should look to find somebody else who can fill that vital role for their children. The establishment of relationships and contact needs to be monitored and managed in the same way as parents monitor any relationships their children develop. The recent media campaign on the issue of paedophilia, while alerting parents to the potential dangers for their children, runs the risk of inhibiting men from exercising many traditional roles lest their motives be thrown open to question. It seems paradoxical that at a time when more fathering is required for our children men are faced with the near-hysteria that surrounds the current debate over paedophilia. Thus while mothers need to be careful they should not forsake the establishment of male-child relationships because of their fear of males who might act with less than honourable intentions.

. . . AND THE LITTLE DAUGHTERS

While there has been much debate about boys' needs for fathering as a result of Steve Biddulph's books, *Manhood* and *Raising Boys*, little discussion has occurred on the question of father-daughter relationships. In both cases it is clear that children who interact with women and men alike grow up more balanced and are less susceptible to many of the problems many young people develop.

While it is important for mothers to try to fill the gap in the lives of their fatherless sons, equal attention should be paid to the needs of daughters so that they too can grow up having experienced a safe and caring relationship with a father figure. This will make them more able to cope with men in their lives and help their confidence and self-esteem to develop.

But finding men to take on some of the roles normally expected of fathers cannot replace a child's love of its natural father, nor should it. These 'big brother' or 'father figure' roles provide at best some opportunity for children to learn about male-child relationships and the importance of men in their lives.

THE PROBLEM OF CHILDLESS FATHERS

The other side of the tragedy of separation is the fathers who now find themselves effectively childless. Some of them may never have seen much of their children in the first place and so now see them for about the same amount of time. While I feel sorry for these men as they get older and start to realise what a mess they have made of their lives, I am more concerned with the loving, caring fathers who now see little of their children.

Unfortunately, if you were to use the popular media as a yardstick, you would conclude that these sorts of fathers do not exist. Fathers are portrayed as either loving at home, unloving but still at home or unloving and separated from their children. Of course, such a simplistic view does not stand up to scrutiny. I know of a number of fathers who are loving, caring men but whose marriages have failed. Consequently they are now separated from their children and they find this separation very difficult.

One man I know was very involved with his kids, taking part in the early morning breakfast ritual and being home for dinner most nights. Following the breakdown of his marriage he now sees them at least every second weekend, but he says: 'Even seeing the kids every weekend is not the same as being there with them every morning, every night. I can see that in some ways they are better off because Mary and I are not fighting any more, but I feel I am losing my kids and there is not a lot I can do about it.'

DIVORCE AND CUSTODY

It remains a matter of concern that we rarely hear of situations like that of my friend. Even with the move to joint parenting decisions (and away from custody battles) fathers in broken marriages are generally destined to accept a lower level of interaction with their children than they may desire. Part of the problem is that men do not expect that they will win custody and so rarely contest it. Some I have spoken to even suggest that deep down they feel that maybe their children will be better off with their mother. They also feel that it would 'not be right' for them to ask for custody and child support even when it is clear that the mother has a much higher earning capacity than the father.

In this instance we are dealing with the legacy of generations of pride and expectations. Fathers deny the fact that they are as capable as single parents as their ex-wives. Thus we need to work to persuade men to stand up and ask for custody and not be swayed by public opinion. There needs to be greater acceptance that men can be just as good as women in bringing up children in single-parent households. Custody should not be automatically awarded to the mother as sometimes tends to be the case today. This means that newly separated fathers need to realise they should play as great a role in their child's development in the future as the mother. We should ensure that they are motivated to want to take their place in this new family structure.

Society's values take time to change and it will be some generations before men start to take a more active role in the day-to-day care of children after divorce. Changes in how men perceive their future role are required, and also in the attitudes of family courts. At this time, however, we need to deal with how to help fathers that are separated from their children. We need to help fathers establish a pattern of involvement with their children that maximises the positive impact a father can have with his children even though he may not live with them. While addressing this issue in the short term is just that—a short-term fix—it does provide a basis that will help ensure fathers stay connected to their children. This in turn will help the child's development as well as the emotional stability of the father.

HOW TO COPE WITH SEPARATION

Fathers faced with the prospect of separation from their children need to think through how to develop their relationship with their children, taking into account the new circumstances. Planning is of primary importance, as is being empathetic with the child's feelings and emotional state. Fathers need to plan the time they will spend with their children not as 'events' but as normal father-child time.

In the spirit of trying to help separated fathers develop strong bonds with their children the following check-list of activities is offered. While they are not meant to be complete, they do provide some direction for fathers wanting to maintain and enhance their relationship with their children after divorce. Of course, even trying to undertake the activities and plans suggested below does not overcome all the problems separated fathers face. These ideas can, however, help them make the best of their situation. The result would hopefully be a continuing strong bond between father and child where both feel fulfilled by the time spent with each other.

- Establish a regular regime that includes time with your children every week. The time should be regularly scheduled so that they can look forward to seeing you. Give these times the same level of importance as any critical work meeting.
- Understand that while your children will always love to go to events and get presents, that is not what provides the basis of a strong bond with them. Furthermore, showering them with gifts and taking them to places or events they would never normally go to can undermine the mother's relationship with them. The father's time should be filled with the same mix of exciting and boring activities as is the mother's time.
- Make sure these scheduled times are long enough to

allow normal social interaction to occur. Allowing ninety minutes with your children is not enough to be valuable, as both you and they will be too aware that time is slipping away.

- Plan on picking your children up from school one day a week. Spend the afternoon doing homework together, attending sports practice, having dinner, playing, talking and finish up by having them stay over (best option) so that you can drop them at school the next day after going through the morning ritual. It is important that this time is seen as normal family time and not hyped up by a bunch of events.

- Spend at least one full weekend every two weeks with your children. Again it is important to treat this as you would normal family time and not as something artificial or forced. Pick them up from school on Friday afternoon and drop them off again on Monday morning. You can always deliver their weekend clothes (washed of course!) to your ex-wife when the kids are at school. Devoting this entire period to them regularly ensures that you have enough time to live normally and not have to force communication with them. Allow them to do the same sort of things during the weekend as they usually would at home, with some slight modifications. Maybe plan a movie, roller-blading or some fun activity on one day. Maybe they play sport on one day or want to see friends. These activities must be allowed to continue. Fathers should not make their children feel guilty if they want to spend some of their 'dad time' with their friends. Spend some of the weekend doing chores with the kids. This is what normal life is about.

- Mix scheduled events with spontaneity. Make regular

arrangements with your ex-wife, but every now and then turn up to pick your child up from school on a day other than your scheduled day (i.e. do two days in that week!).

- Make the time to understand how your children are doing at school. Continue (or start!) to be involved in school activities so that you remain connected to your children's school life. Don't just turn up for formal school events. Attend these but get more involved in other things as well.

- Take a similar interest in their out-of-school activities. Coach their soccer or netball teams. Officiate at Little Athletics or Nippers. Take on a formal role with your children's sport or hobbies so that they see you being involved and they begin to expect it to continue.

- Make the time to know your children's friends and their parents. This will be difficult in many situations where your ex-wife and your children's friends' parents are friends, but you have a right to know as much about your children's lives as their mother so bear with the difficulty.

- Persevere. Working your life so that you can be with your children for enough time to make a difference requires patience, energy and commitment. Never give up and never let yourself slip into a mode where you begin to question the value of what you bring to your children and to yourself. Having large amounts of time with them will help you influence their development and it will also show them how much you love them. In turn spending this time with them will help you.

THE BOY WHOSE PARENTS COULDN'T CARE LESS

I want to close this short chapter with a story about an incident at my eldest child's school some years ago.

My wife and I arrived to pick up our daughter at the end of the day and also to attend a regular parent-teacher meeting which was being held that afternoon. As we entered the administration block I noticed a young boy about ten years old sitting outside the principal's office looking very dejected. I couldn't help wondering what had happened to him.

When we came out of the meeting some thirty minutes later, the boy was still there. Apparently the boy came from a broken home and the day in question it was the father's turn to pick up the child from school, but he hadn't come. When the boy rang his mother from the admin office to ask what was happening, she screamed about what a deadbeat the father was and hung up. He then rang his father, who went on about what a witch the mother was and how it was actually her turn to pick him up. Eventually, just before we left, the father arrived and drove the boy away. When I heard the explanation my heart went out to the young boy. It was not his fault that his parents no longer loved each other. All he wanted was to be picked up from school like any normal kid and not have to go through the humiliation of being stuck in the admin block while his parents sorted out who had screwed up.

There is so much wrong with how the parents acted in this situation. Both acted irresponsibly and inflicted great pain on their child. Firstly, they should have been absolutely clear on who was responsible for the boy that afternoon and whichever one it was should have met the commitment. Secondly, the parents had no right to inflict their dislike of each other on the child and take out their frustration on him. If one parent had forgotten the other should have understood how the boy was feeling and rushed over to the school and collected him.

WRAPPING UP

Family breakdowns are a reality: people change and marriages collapse. While divorce can help the parents and also some children, where tensions in the marriage spilled over into emotional and physical impact on the children, we need to give some special thought to the plight of children left fatherless by marriage break-up as well as for the fathers who are left predominantly childless. Children need the ongoing support of a father, but equally fathers also need their children in order to be complete men. They need the opportunity to nurture, develop and protect their children. They also need the regular flow of love and affection that children and parents can offer each other when there is a strong, deep bond between them.

9

I want to be a better dad for my kids and myself ...

T he main premise of this book is that fathers are not spending enough time with their children. This is the result of changes in society and the values we tend to live by. Time with children alone is not the whole story, however. To get to a situation where a father would consciously choose to be separated by his work from his children for much of their lives calls into question our work ethic and our understanding of our roles as parents.

Moreover, the time with children yardstick also indicates to what extent fathers have let work take over their lives. It is not surprising to find that fathers who are too busy to spend time with their children are also too busy to spend time with their wives and friends or invest time in any hobby. Thus, while my concern is more about the father-child relationship and how it has been affected by work, there are many more tragedies that occur because of the same disease. Marriage breakdown, losing lifelong friends and ending up retired with nothing in one's life bar work memories are just some of the disasters brought about by our acceptance of increased work time as being a good and honourable way to focus our energies.

WE ALL KNOW WHAT WE OUGHT TO DO

Interestingly, we rarely hear of an elderly man, wrapping up the loose ends of his life, talking about how he wishes he had worked harder and spent more hours away from his family. Variations of this example abound and yet we continue to work as many hours as ever. Surely this suggests that something is very, very wrong with how we are leading our lives. The fact that nearly everyone we hear of who has gone through a life-threatening experience comes out the other end making radical changes to his or her life should tell us something. The people 'fortunate' enough to have been woken up from their work-induced coma are suddenly able, with incredible clarity, to see how screwed-up their lives had become and they immediately plan changes. More time with family, more time on hobbies and interests. Why? Because these other parts of life are actually the things that really matter, combined with a work environment that allows people to develop and deliver on their skills.

So people who have lost someone dear to them or have suffered some close call with death change their lives, or at least talk about changing their lives. This tells us everything we need to know about planning our lives for the future. We know that when work priorities are objectively compared to life priorities and when we get over the belief that more money will transform our lives, all of us seem to come up with the same basic ideas for changing our lives. It's quite amazing that people are so consistent. The responses to such wake-up calls don't form a random graph covering everything from wanting to spend more time at work through to more time shopping. Instead people make it clear they want to spend more time with their family and friends and generally enjoy life. Yet despite this overwhelming evidence we still go back to our empty work-oriented lives. The fact that we do not change our lives and reject the work-value system that has been created is testament to the power of work as an influencing agent. So much of our self-esteem and sense of purpose is tied up with work that we seem unable to distinguish between the role work should play in our lives and the importance of other aspects.

Death by a Thousand Cuts

- **Your child is hurt in an accident. There is no question as to where you should be. You rush from work to be with the child at the hospital. Work colleagues drive you to make sure you get there in one piece.**
- **Your child expects you to come to the swimming carnival but at the last moment you let a work meeting take precedence. You don't turn up. Nobody at work questions your decision. But your child is upset.**

In the first example the child was physically in danger and you wanted to be with it. In the second you chose to hurt your child by dismissing important events in its life as being secondary to your work. **Why do we all agree with the father's actions in the first scenario but have differing ideas about those in the second? Is the distinction the fact that the child's life was in danger in the former case, but not in the latter? But there is a sense in which the child's life is in danger in the second example. Of course, missing one swimming carnival is not a telling blow. However, as a part of a regular pattern it becomes a stage in death by a thousand cuts, each one hurting that little bit more. Overall the child realises it doesn't rate with its father and the love between them has died. Waking up years later will not help the father, trying to repair the relationship: re-stranding the rope that bound him and his child will not work. It's over. Perhaps if the child is a caring person it will accept whatever love it can get from its father and yet both know that theirs will not be a relationship of closeness—and they both weep at their loss.**

TIME FOR CHANGE AT THE TOP

The previous chapters have dealt with different aspects of the life of a father in corporate life. The examples used are drawn from the world of the business executive because it is a world I know well and one which sets a pattern of behaviour which is then replicated throughout companies and industries at large. If the attitudes and actions of our corporate leaders could be changed then we would have a better society. It will not come through government programs because the people who need to be influenced are those who chase money as their measure of success. They have to show the way.

- We need leaders of these companies to stand up and say they really do think that families are more important than work and that you can be successful in their organisation by working hard for forty or fifty hours and not more.
- We need leaders to lead by example, go home early enough to spend time with their children, take time out of the working day to attend a school reading program or some similar parent-helper activity.
- We need to start to structure our business day assuming that people will want to go home and spend time with their family.
- We need to look to promote individuals who not only perform well in the work environment but who are also good fathers, husbands and community members. Obsessed workaholics should not be rewarded for their dedication. They should be moved sideways while they undergo detox for their addiction.

SURVIVING FROM CRISIS TO CRISIS

I know of many executives whose jobs are really a set of major crises jammed together. They leap from one very important, tightly time-framed project to another. Sacrifices in family time are made 'just at this time because I am working to get this bid in on time'. Win or lose, these people rarely look back and determine what the costs to their family were for the time given to the 'project'. Increasingly I have found that downtime between these major projects or bids is shorter and shorter. The rhetoric of 'taking time to make up with the family once the project is over' no longer translates into any serious time with the family because before you can blink another major project/

bid/opportunity requires a return to workaholic time commitments. The words remain the same and perhaps there exists even some sense of commitment, but the delivery to the family is always sacrificed.

What makes this type of behaviour so depressing is the people who are affected by the workaholic executive. Of course, the children and wife suffer, but as I have mentioned previously so does the executive. He is not aware at the time, while he is caught in the momentum of business, but as sure as night follows day he will suffer. One day when the game of business has stopped or the executive is no longer quite as necessary to the company as he thought he was the suffering will begin. He will realise that he has thrown away the one opportunity to build a relationship of love, care and friendship with his child. While spousal relationships and close friendships are equally important, nothing can take the place of a relationship with your child. In the same way that many executives suffer deep grief when they lose their wives through neglect, they will suffer grief at the lost opportunity with their children.

A senior executive from one of my ex-employers was quoted as saying: 'There are five crusades that our employees will live and die by this financial year'. This came from a man who has perhaps 2,000 people working for him. Unfortunately I think he believes that his employees should really 'live and die' for the company's financial goals. Of equal concern was the way the press dealt with this remark. Nowhere was it suggested that this man is lacking balance. Nowhere was it stated that someone in such a key position who espouses such ideas should be taken out of his role and counselled before he is ever allowed to manage people again.

As we have seen earlier, executives in charge of large complex businesses easily get roped into committing their lives to the company and its success. More often than not they are moulding themselves on previous or current senior managers or they are behaving in accordance with how they think they should act. Their initial dedication to wanting to do a good job is both admirable and under-standable, but if allowed to go unchecked it runs the risk of turning into megalomania. Their inability to retain a sense of balance is the first sign of worse to come.

In a world led by the work-obsessed, as we have today, we can't expect the organisations themselves to suddenly change their approach or value systems. Nor can we expect that magically hundreds of senior executives will realise overnight how screwed-up their lives are and start to make wholesale changes both in their lives and in the way they operate their companies. Change of the kind which will help our society will only come through the actions of indi-viduals, at all levels of an organisation, working to their own plan and not one which is delivered to them by their employer. Individuals who want to wait for organisational approval before they change their lives will need to be pre-pared for a long wait. Moreover, change will probably come much too late to affect their own lives.

STRATEGIES FOR SUCCESS

This phrase is often used in business texts and speeches to introduce a set of steps that companies should take in order to achieve a better commercial performance. In this book I talk about success as being the living of a life which is complete in all areas, where an individual has worked hard in his career, his marital relationship, the development of his children, his friendships and his community.

You have had a successful life if you have tried your best in each of these areas. If you have concentrated your energies on only one aspect then your life is not a success. It has been out of balance, as a result of which you have not accomplished what was expected of you. Being successful in business does not make up for being an absent father or disinterested member of the community.

You can be successful in business while also being a great father, husband and community member. In fact, 'being a success' should require achievement in career, family, personal and community areas. The most admirable business leaders are those who achieve financial success for their organisations while:

- being an involved father and spouse;
- investing energy and resources into community activities;
- building organisations which have developed a work culture which respects and values the family, prioritises family issues appropriately to work goals and provides leadership to other companies in Australia; and
- maintaining an active interest in some personal pursuits.

I have always maintained that you can achieve significant business success while also being an involved father and spouse and being active in the community. But if you want to maximise business or career success then you can't also be an involved father. You can be a success in business but MAXIMUM SUCCESS requires complete dedication. One has to question whether maximum success is necessary or desirable. It is simply not possible to work excessive hours, devote total energy to work and then also have the time and energy to be a good father. Thus a key skill is being able to determine how much business success or effort is enough so that energy and resources can be devoted to other priorities.

This requires an executive to approach work and the delivery of goals in a manner which maximises efficiency of effort and not quantity of effort. It also requires the executive to be able to know when 'enough is enough'. If working hard achieves 100 per cent of your goals for the company and yourself, is it right to invest the further effort to get to an achievement of 130 per cent of your financial and performance goals?

Of course, companies will try to motivate their employees to over-achieve. In this as leaders we are all irresponsible. We are motivating people to devote as much time and effort as possible to work. Smart executives will see life as a marathon race where meeting your goals (achieving 100 per cent each year and having time for your family) is far more important than spending a number of years over-achieving and thus neglecting your family. To repeat, your family will not wait for you to be successful and then allow you to take up where you left off. Be very conscious of the choice you make every day in terms of time lost, and lost forever, for your family. There is *never* a make-up time. Time can't be borrowed back or stacked up for future use.

A Plan for Action

Outlined below are a number of strategies and actions which can help you focus on being a better father. For any of them to be of use there has to first be at least some level of acceptance that a balanced life is desirable and some degree of support for the premise that fathers should spend more time with their children. If you still find the concept of the pursuit of balance not worth supporting then these strategies will not help you. For those who still see some virtue in the father being a remote figure detached from the everyday life of his children, I would suggest that unfortunately a wake-up call might be your only salvation. If you believe that your child's development is in no way affected by the amount of time you spend with them please stop having kids. We have enough children who have been adversely affected by selfish parents as it is.

For those who are beginning to question the career road they are travelling I offer the following strategies for success. They worked for me and hopefully they will work, in some form, for you. They encompass taking an inventory of your life, understanding the different periods of fathering, understanding that life is a long journey, establishing life goals, being prepared to take control of your life and using time away to remind yourself of what is important.

TAKING A LIFE INVENTORY

Take some time to reflect on your life. Before you can start to plan a future set of activities you have to have a very clear view of where you are starting. Review all aspects of your life and the decisions you have made on the way. Be honest in your analysis. In Chapter 2 a framework for structuring forward planning was outlined. This can only be applied once you have taken a full and honest inventory of your life. Make a list of answers to the following questions and then review them to determine areas requiring attention.

Family

- Do you fit your family commitments around your work commitments?
- Does your family think you put them ahead of work or the other way around?
- Have you been as good a husband as you wanted to be?
- Does your wife think you have been the sort of partner she thought she was marrying? If not why not?
- What have you done recently to enhance your relationship with your wife?
- Have you been as good a father as you wanted to be?
- What would your children say about you as a father?
- Are you spending as much time as you want to with your children?

Career

- Are you at the level you want to be in your career?

- What do you want in a career that you do not have now?
- Are you prepared to sacrifice aspects of your life for your career? Why?
- Do you respect your managers in terms of their approach to life as well as work?

Personal

- Do you have any interests or hobbies that you spend time on when your wife, children and work colleagues are not involved?
- Are there things you have always wanted to do but have never allocated time for? Learning a musical instrument, painting, or taking up a new sport, for example.
- Do you feel you have lost your sense of identity to that created by your work situation and family demands?

DIFFERENT PERIODS OF FATHERING

The early years with a child are the ones when they will need you most and they will want you more. From birth to approximately the age of eight or nine a child will be very much connected to the parent. Obviously in its first few weeks and months a child will get to know the sound of its parents' voices and their touch and smell. A baby is not awake for very long periods and the father's interaction is limited to bathing, feeding and consoling it when it is crying. Very quickly, though, the child develops a relation-ship with the parent, given the parent has spent the time to develop the relationship.

As the child grows it will use its parents as both a source of safety as well as a reference point for everything that is going on in the world. During these early learning years the child will often defer to its parents in terms of what is good and bad. Through the parents' life the child will experience new foods, new places and new concepts. Parents play an extremely influential role in these early years— influential if they are around. If not the child will seek out other reference points to use.

As the child continues to grow it starts to turn away from its parents as the primary influence. Of course, if the relationship is strong enough, it will come back in search of more direction or advice. If the basis of a strong relationship is not in place by this time then as the child grows it will be increasingly difficult for the parent to establish a deep relationship with it. I have heard many fathers talk about how they can't relate to babies or toddlers, but when 'Harry is ten or eleven then I will be able to relate to him'. This is just a cop-out. Communication with young children is not easy for most people. Most fathers and mothers have had little experience with this type of interaction prior to having kids. It is up to both parents to develop these skills. Fathers who wait until their children are 'older' in terms of developing a relationship with them have lost the opportunity forever.

Unfortunately the timing of young children tends to coincide with the time in your career when you are attempting to make the great leap forward. Both require significant time commitment and neither the career nor young children will necessarily wait around for attention. On balance it is far more important to ensure that time is given to young children than allocating more time to your career because you only have one chance with your children whereas you can afford to delay the progress of your career a little.

It is critical to allocate time to your child in their early years especially. This means time every day in keeping with the pattern described earlier—some time every day with long periods at weekends and on holidays. When introducing children to new activities, make sure that the ones you choose are things you can both engage in. It is also important to pay attention to what is going on. Too often you see children with parents who are obviously not taking any interest in them. Children will ask questions and want you to join in a game. Answer the questions to the best of your ability and take up the opportunity to play a game because it will not be long before they won't want you to play. Besides, it's good fun.

The early years are also a time when a child will take what you say as the truth. In many cases what we say is only our opinion and not fact. Be mindful of the influence you have and if your child wants to discuss some issue where the truth is not always so clear (politics, religion, etc), make sure you try to give it a balanced view. By making it clear that it is only your opinion, you are also giving the child some early lessons in making up its own mind.

LIFE AS A JOURNEY

When you plan a long journey, you spend time thinking about where you want to go, how you want to get there, where you will get supplies along the way, what you want to see and of course making sure you get there. Life is no different except that, surprisingly, most people do not plan their lives at all, never having much more than a very short view of the future.

If you live your life with a short-term view, you will make decisions that make sense in terms of your current position, but not in terms of your whole life. People caught up in the daily grind, responding to daily requests from their employers and little more, will more often than not trade off things that do not provide short-term gain. Taking time away from the family and devoting it to work is an example of this type of trade-off. The only way to try to get focused on the fact that in the long term you will want a good relationship with your wife and children is to take a whole-of-life view. This perspective also ensures that you keep a good sense of what life is all about.

Being busy is no excuse for not having a plan. Not having at least some form of plan for your life is a cop-out. By not planning you are not only letting your family down but also yourself. Planning your life also requires you to think about life and its many dimensions. A life plan is not a career plan. A career plan is part of a life plan.

LIFE GOALS

As has been mentioned earlier, you need to set goals for all parts of your life. Establish a set of five-year goals for your family, career, financial status and personal interests. Then evaluate these goals in terms of the progress you have made in three years and then one year. In this way you will be able to test whether on your current track you are in line to achieve your five-year goals. If not, then you have a choice: take action that will get you back on track to your goals, change your goals to make them more achievable with your current direction or continue to live your life as a lie—aspiring for some goals in the future but doing nothing about them.

In establishing these goals the following framework may help. Please note that family goals are more important than career, financial and personal goals, though I accept in some cases these are related.

Family goals

- Establish a number of hours per day that you want to spend with your child and spouse;
- Define some holiday that you want to take your family on;
- Define some interest or hobby which the family will take on as a group interest;
- Undertake to be at school (outside of events) for one morning per term;
- Take time to be with each of your children individually so that the two of you can share some time;
- Think about how you are influencing your child's thinking and whether you are being as balanced as you can.

Career goals

- What job do you want to be in five years from now and what jobs will you need to have in three years' time and in fact next year to give you a chance of achieving this five-year goal?
- What skills do you need to develop to remain marketable and promotable?
- To what extent do your career goals allow you to achieve

your family goals? If you are trading off the family, why? Set career goals that allow more balance between them and your family goals.

- What sort of company culture do you want to work in? What steps can you take to achieve this?

Financial status

- What are your financial goals five years from now? What are these goals based on? To what extent are your goals based on needs or a desire to 'keep up with the Joneses'? Can you tell the difference?
- Are the goals achievable given your current income? Does your current income require you to work hours that are destroying your family?
- Do your financial goals conform to your career and family goals? If not then change your financial goals and career goals first.

Personal interests

In this book I have not, perhaps, spent enough time discussing the need for personal time. A full life needs to be made up of work, family time and personal time. If any of these areas are neglected then the life is not whole and is by definition unbalanced. I would go so far as to say that to be a good dad you have to have some time where you focus on personal interests. By allocating this time you bring to your children new skills and interests, you show them that life is about doing things that you enjoy and you are more likely to give them truly focused time when you are with them.

It is important for people to have their own time—time to spend on activities which involve their own interests and do not necessarily include other family members. This time should not be at the expense of the family. The executive who works a seventy-hour week and then *has* to play golf all day Saturday and sail on Sunday is abusing the concept of personal time. Do something every week that you want to do, but do not trade off significant family time to do this. Trade off work time.

- What interests would you like to develop over the next five years?
- Map out the time required to develop these skills without trading off significant family time. If you can't achieve the time required developing the skills, then look to trade off work time.
- Are your interests a mix of those which help the mind and the body? It's a good idea to work on both.
- Are your interests inherently anti-family? Do they take you away from home too often or motivate you to act in a way that negatively affects your family? If so find some other interest. When you are single is the time for these pursuits, not when you have a family. Anything that takes you away from your family for a whole day on the weekend every weekend should be left to single people or married people with no children.

TAKING CONTROL OF YOUR LIFE

As has been stated a number of times, you have to take control of your own life. You can't live your life at the beck and call of anyone else or any organisation. Never let your company effectively control your life. If it does, find a company or career where you can get back control. Do not trade money for control. Giving up control of your life for more money is not unlike Faust playing with the devil. Nothing is for free. If you trade control for money, while you may have money you will have paid for the loss of control in other ways—such as losing your family—a big price to pay to fund a new car or larger house.

Taking control of your life also means you have to have a plan (see above) and you have to develop your own set of values built on what you truly believe in and not what you are told to believe in by your peers or your employer or manager. Equally, question values that are passed on by past generations. Test them to see whether they reflect how you want your life to be judged and measured. Think a lot about how your family would describe you and the life you are leading. 'Dad worked very long hours and we never saw much of him, but we got to attend an exclusive private school' is not a positive endorsement of your life choices. Equally, 'Dad was never around but he built this really successful company' is not a good measure of your life.

TAKING TIME AWAY

It is often very hard to think clearly when you are caught up in the daily rush between work and home. Existing is not living and being active does not mean you are making progress. To really get a handle on how your life is going requires you to take time away and to do nothing but think. Take at least one day a year to spend by yourself, away from home, away from work, away from friends or personal interests. Spend the day thinking about your life, about all its parts and about where it is going. This time can also be spent taking an inventory as was described above as well as to think about your goals for the future. It is also very useful to play back in your mind interactions with family and friends over the past year.

Think through how you reacted to situations, what you said or didn't say. Were you reacting as the person you are deep down or as the work guy who is momentarily distracted by something else? Are you proud of how you acted? Embed in your mind lessons from these interactions—lessons on how to behave and how to respond to your friends and family.

Taking time away is a frightening prospect for most people, because it provides a space which lets your mind wander. You can't hide behind a busy schedule or an activity that requires significant concentration. Initially time will drag, as your mind learns again to wander through issues and through past experiences. But soon the time away will allow you to return clearer on where you want your life to go and how to interact with those whom you care about.

IN THE END

Wake up calls are very powerful motivators for change. I would not, however, want everyone to receive the type of calls that I described earlier in this book. Some level of change can perhaps come in the form of mini-wake-up calls, developed expressly for the busy executive of today. If you are not sure whether you have your head properly centred in terms of life and the balance between work and family try a couple of these mini-wake-up calls:

- Pick up your baby and place your nose on the top of its head. Breathe deeply and inhale the smell of babies. It is a unique smell which, if you let it, pervades your body and fills it with a sense of love and calm. You also feel very much in touch with what is really important in life.

- Go into your older children's room when they are asleep and sit on the edge of their beds and watch them asleep. Look at their peaceful sleep and their serenity. Think back to how recently it seemed that they were little babies and yet here they are young persons bordering on adulthood. Bend down and give them a kiss on the cheek and remember back to the time when they were born and you pledged your love and care.

- Find some old photos of your wife which were taken soon after your marriage. Stare at the photo and think back to the love you had for her at the time and how much she meant to you. Think about what you have done recently to repay your wife for her devotion and love. Or did you forget that she was there and that she loved you more than life itself?

- Look in the mirror, straight after waking up in the morning. You're not getting younger. Life is not a dress rehearsal for something else that happens next time around. Look deeply into your own eyes and tell yourself this is it. This is your life and you are living it the way *you* want. If you're not then change it before the bloke in the mirror gets any older.

- Leave work one day early enough to drop by your child's kindergarten and watch the kids play in the playground. Listen to their laughter and watch their smiles. Marvel at their energy levels. Remember back to a time when you were young enough to laugh often during a day, race around with unlimited energy or just wander around happy to be out on a sunny day. We can learn a lot from watching children. At a basic level we can learn about taking life and enjoying it. Everyone has a child inside him and everyone wants to laugh and smile.

A FINAL WRAP

With three children spanning an eight-year gap, I have the privilege of talking to one daughter about Switchfoot's latest album, selecting a fashion accessory for another and helping the third develop a new cool Bratz doll board game, all in the space of a few hours.

I regularly think back to when they were born and those first moments of holding them. The rush of emotions, the angst as to whether I was up to being the father they deserved, my dedication to nurture them and help them on their life journey. And yet this commitment to them and their lives does not suggest you can't have equally lofty ambitions for your career.

My work both with commercial and not-for-profit organisations remains very important to me. My work helps define who I am and it gives me a greater sense of purpose and self-esteem. Without work I do feel a lack of a sense of belonging. I am sure that work is no less important to me than to any other father in the workforce. I am very conscious, however, of my priorities and I do try to ensure my family's needs come first.

While work allows me to use my skills and develop new ones it will never again be the most important 'thing' in my life. There will be times when I will have to work more than 50 hours a week, but these times are rare and will remain so. To generate the balance I have in my life I have made choices which have perhaps meant I did not go 'as far' as I could have gone in my career. The trade-off that I made was a very easy choice—greater career success with less family involvement or moderate career success and a strong family life. It's not even a discussion worth having, actually, as the decision seems so obvious.

Throughout this book I have tried to develop a theme using research I have carried out during my permanently stalled PhD and drawing on my personal experiences to suggest that an unhealthy work commitment undermines the family. I firmly believe that the family is the most important 'thing' people will have in their lives and like any living thing it needs attention and care. It is my experience that business leaders generally may talk a lot about how important their family is but in practice they are in love with their work and everything else comes second. This value system is twisted and yet these leaders go on to develop organisations in which their work ethic pervades every level of their structures.

So how do I rate my performance as a father against the ideas and models outlined in this book?

I think I was able to take corrective action in my life before my work obsession caused irreparable damage to my family. I have tried to balance my career desires, time with my wife, time with my children and personal time. Balancing has simply meant being very strict with my diary and ensuring work does not grow beyond its allotted hours in any week. This may sound simple and it actually is. The difficult part is letting yourself take control and not letting work take control. I make sure that family time in my diary has the same level of importance as work meetings. I find the only way to make sure I spend the time I want with the family is to have my diary reflect my true life plan. Experience has shown me that if your diary only reflects work commitments then you will not be able to meet your commitments to your family. Of course this often leads to conflict but over time I have made sure those I work with understand where my priorities lie.

Not so surprisingly I have found that my performance at work has not suffered and I have yet to find a meeting or commitment that could not be managed around family commitments.

Where I know I am failing is in the area of personal time. The next stage of my development will require me to feel OK about doing things for myself. Currently if I am not at work I feel I should be with my kids. If I do things for myself I feel guilty. I can see the problem and am working on it.

Generally, with this issue understood, I can say that I have truly done my best in terms of trying to be a good father, husband, friend, community member and employee. Basically that is all one can aspire to and thus I feel a high level of contentment with my life to date. Sure there is room for improvement but that again is what life is all about.

In closing let me be even more purposefully repetitive. Children need their fathers. They need their fathers around them every day. This is not speculation. It is a proven fact. You can choose to ignore this fact and you can choose to dismiss my comments as being unrealistic. If you are leading a life that is work-dominated and you still feel as though you are doing a great job as a father and husband then I challenge you to stop for just a moment and really think about the direction your life is taking. If you stay on your course perhaps one day you may get a wake-up call—loud and piercing—which will maybe make you see that you have been caught up in a cruel and binding hoax. At that time you will perhaps see what this book is all about.

To be an involved father you do not need to work part-time, have a successful international career or be of any particular profession or trade. Being involved in your children's life requires only that you think deeply about the sort of father you want to be and then what small changes (as hard as they may initially seem) you can make to improve your relationship with them. The greater involvement you have the more likely you will be able to help them as they navigate life and the more likely they will turn to you for guidance and for a shoulder to lean on. Being an involved father requires only a few hours a week of focused effort and a commitment to being part of your child's activities, schooling and social development.

Before judging my comments, however, I would ask you to sit quietly, drop your guard and really think about your life, how you have treated your family and how you are living your life. When darkness falls and you are alone, are you really happy with your life and how you are living it? If not, then change your life, starting now. Do it for yourself and for your family.

References and further reading

Biddulph, Steve, *Manhood*, Finch, 1993.

—, *Raising Boys*, Finch, 1997.

Birch, Charles and Paul, David, *Life and Work*, UNSW Press, 2003.

Boyle, David, *The Sum of our Discontent*, Texere, New York, 2001.

Burgess, Adrienne, *Fatherhood Reclaimed*, Vermilian, 1997.

Collins, Jim, *Good to Great*, Random House, New York, 2001.

Eckersley, Richard, *Well & Good*, Text Publishing, 2004.

Evans, P. and Bartoleme, F., 'Professional Lives vs Private Lives: Shifting Patterns of Management Commitment,' *Organisational Dynamics*, Vol 7, No 4, 1979.

Glezer, H., 'Juggling Work and Family Commitments,' *Family Matters*, AIFS, 1991.

Goleman, Daniel, *Emotional Intelligence*, Bloomsbury Publishing, 1996.

Hochschild, Arlie Russell, *The Time Bind*, Henry Holt, 1997.

Hood, Jane, *Men, Work and Family*, Sage, 1993.

Joyce, William, Nohira, Nitin and Roberson, Bruce, *What Really Works*, Harper Business, 2003.

Kotter, John and Heskett, James, *Corporate Culture and Performance*, Free Press, 1992.

Lencioni, Patrick, 'Make Your Values Mean Something', *Harvard Business Review*, July 2000.

Maister, David, *Practice What You Preach*, Free Press, 2002.

Maslow, Abraham, *Maslow on Management*, Wiley and Sons, 1998.

O'Neill, John, *The Paradox of Success*, McGraw-Hill, 1993.

Parsons, Rob, *Heart of Success*, Hodder & Stoughton, 2002.

Pleck, J.H. and Lamb, M.E., 'Facilitating Future Changes: Men's Family roles,' in Lewis, R.A. and Sussman, M. (eds), *Men's Changing Roles in the Family*, Howarth, 1985.

Russell, G., Savage, G. and Durkin, K., 'Balancing Work and Family: An Emerging Issue for Private and Public Sector Organisations,' unpublished paper, School of Behavioural Sciences, Macquarie University, 1995.

Schein, E.H., *Organisational Culture and Leadership*, 2nd ed. Jossey-Bass, 1997.

Weiss, R.S., *Staying the Course*, The Free Press, New York, 1990.

Acknowledgments

I have been fortunate to be married to a most wonderful woman, Carolyn, for the last eighteen years. Together we have produced three beautiful daughters (Grace, Eliza and Alice). Carolyn turned an obsessed workaholic into someone who saw there was more to life. For this and for everything else she has given of herself I am eternally grateful.

I thank my daughters for their unconditional love and for sharing their lives with me.

I would like to thank Jane Curry for her tremendous support over the years. What started as a casual conversation in 1995 has blossomed into four books and, moreover, a joint commitment to try to bring to the fore some of the issues that are a function of the ever-expanding role of work in our society.

Finally, my thanks to Steve Biddulph, Shaaron Biddulph, Jack Heath, Shane Thompson, John Treloar, Aidan Grimes, Rob Olver, Cathy Treloar and Carolyn. Without the help of these friends the project would never have come together quite as well as it seems to have.